The Authentic Mediterranean Diet Cookbook for Beginners

2000 Days of Quick and Nutritious Mediterranean Recipes for Weight Loss, Heart Health, and Longevity, 28-Day Meal Plan for Healthy Eating on a Budget

Brenda A. Howell

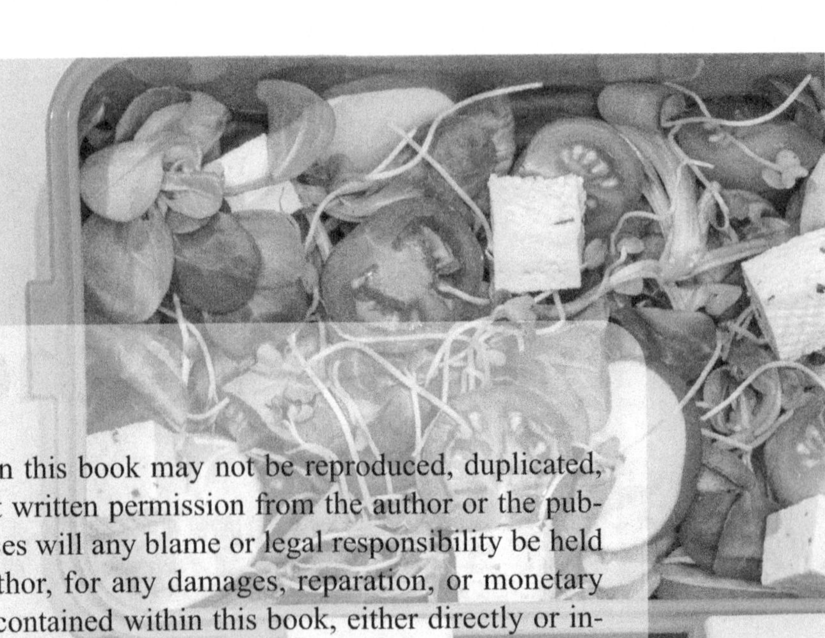

CONTENTS

INTRODUCTION

Brenda A. Howell, a seasoned traveler and passionate chef, has meticulously curated a collection that pays homage to the sun-kissed shores of the Mediterranean, encapsulating its rich history, diverse culture, and unparalleled culinary heritage. Drawing inspiration from her own adventures across the Mediterranean coasts and her encounters with local cooks and food enthusiasts, she presents a tapestry of dishes that are as nutritious as they are delectable.

This cookbook is more than just a collection of recipes; it's an invitation to embrace a lifestyle that has been celebrated for its wellness benefits and heartwarming simplicity. Each page unfolds the secrets of the Mediterranean diet, a harmonious blend of olive oil, fresh produce, grains, and lean proteins, enlivened with robust herbs and spices.

Whether you're a novice in the kitchen or a seasoned chef, Brenda's personal anecdotes, preparation tips, and cultural snippets ensure that you're not just preparing a meal but immersing yourself in a rich cultural experience. From hearty mains to refreshing salads, from age-old traditional dishes to contemporary classics, this cookbook promises a repertoire that will satiate both the soul and the senses.

So, open the pages, indulge in the vivid photography, and let Brenda A. Howell guide you to creating and enjoying the finest Mediterranean delicacies in the comfort of your home. To good health, timeless traditions, and unforgettable meals.

Who is the Mediterranean diet more suitable for?

Heart Health Seekers

The diet is renowned for its cardiovascular benefits. People looking to manage their blood pressure, cholesterol levels, or overall heart health can benefit from adopting this diet.

Weight Managers

Those aiming to lose or maintain weight can find the Mediterranean diet beneficial due to its emphasis on whole foods, healthy fats, and fiber-rich ingredients that can keep one satiated.

Diabetics

The Mediterranean diet can be beneficial for people with type 2 diabetes as it promotes blood sugar control and has been shown to reduce the risk of diabetic complications.

Cancer Risk Reducers

Some studies suggest that the Mediterranean diet might help reduce the risk of certain types of cancers, mainly due to its high content of antioxidants, phytonutrients, and anti-inflammatory properties.

Brain Health Enthusiasts

Individuals concerned about cognitive decline, Alzheimer's disease, or dementia might benefit since the diet has been associated with improved brain health and function.

Gut Health Focused

With its emphasis on fiber and diverse plant foods, the Mediterranean diet supports a healthy gut microbiome, potentially benefiting those with digestive concerns.

General Health Advocates

Even for those without specific health concerns, the Mediterranean diet is a sensible choice for promoting overall wellbeing, longevity, and prevention of chronic diseases.

Lovers of Flavor

Beyond health reasons, those who simply enjoy flavorful, fresh, and diverse foods might be naturally drawn to the Mediterranean way of eating.

Common ingredients of the Mediterranean diet

- **Fruits and Vegetables**

These form a significant part of the Mediterranean diet. Staple fruits include citrus fruits, berries, grapes, figs, and apples. Key vegetables range from leafy greens like spinach and kale to other vegetables such as tomatoes, cucumbers, bell peppers, zucchinis, eggplants, and more.

- **Whole Grains**

Whole grains like whole wheat, oats, barley, brown rice, and ancient grains like quinoa and farro are essential for their fiber content and sustained energy release.

- **Legumes and Nuts**

Legumes like lentils, chickpeas, and various kinds of beans are commonly used in Mediterranean recipes. Nuts and seeds, such as almonds, walnuts, sunflower seeds, and sesame seeds, are also integral parts of the diet.

- **Olive Oil**

Perhaps the most iconic ingredient, olive oil is a primary source of fat in the Mediterranean diet, used in cooking and in dressings for salads and dips.

- **Seafood**

The Mediterranean diet encourages regular consumption of fish, particularly fatty fish like salmon, mackerel, sardines, and tuna for their high omega-3 content.

- **Herbs and Spices**

These are used in abundance to add flavor to dishes, reducing the need for added salt. This includes herbs and spices like garlic, basil, oregano, rosemary, thyme, and dill, among others.

- **Cheese and Yogurt**

Dairy products, particularly those from sheep and goats, are commonly consumed in the Mediterranean diet. These include feta, ricotta, and Greek yogurt.

- **Poultry and Eggs**

While red meat is limited in the Mediterranean diet, poultry, eggs, and other sources of lean protein are consumed moderately.

- **Wine**

Moderate consumption of red wine is often associated with the Mediterranean diet, always taken with meals and never in excess.

- **Olives and Capers**

Olives, both green and black, along with capers, are widely used for their unique flavor and health benefits.

What cuisines does the Mediterranean Diet cookbook offer?

Appetizers & Small Plates: Delightful starters that set the tone for a Mediterranean feast, such as bruschettas, mezze platters

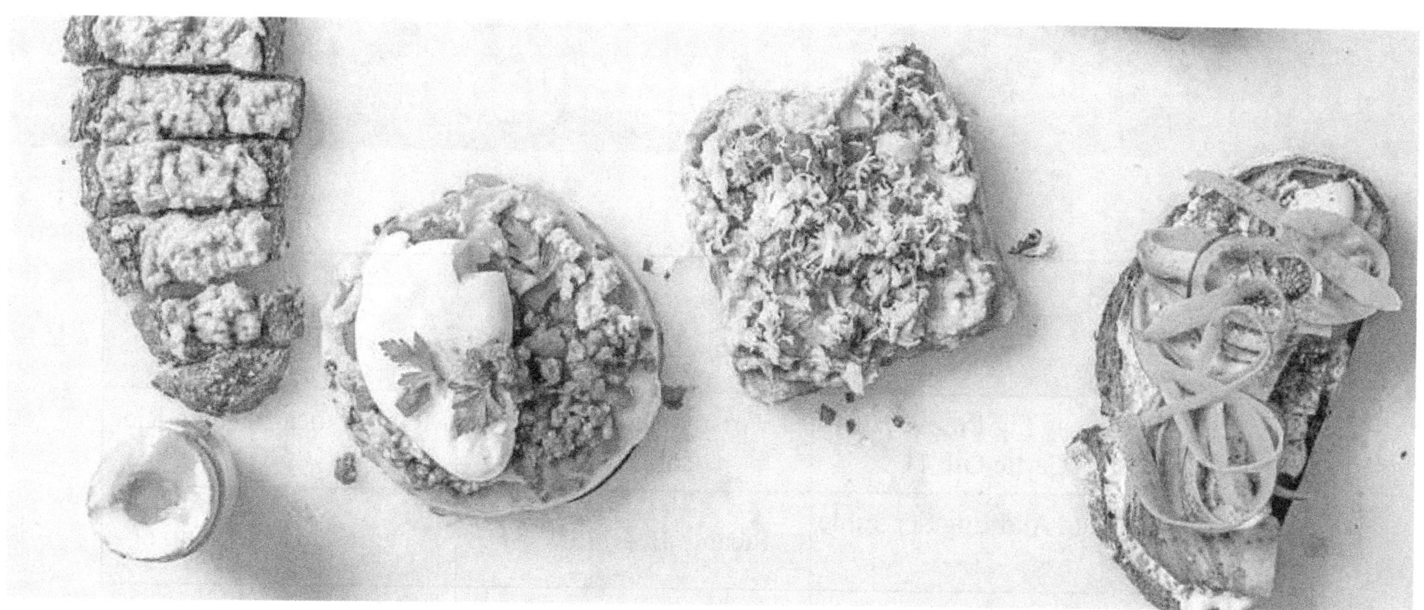

Soups & Broths: Hearty and wholesome soups like Spanish gazpacho, Turkish lentil soup, and Italian minestrone.

Salads & Cold Dishes: Refreshing salads using fresh produce, olives, and cheeses, including favorites like Nicoise salad, Greek salad, and fattoush.

Seafood Delicacies: The Mediterranean is known for its seafood dishes, and this section might feature plates such as Spanish paella, Sicilian swordfish rolls, and grilled sardines.

Vegetarian & Plant-Based Recipes: Highlighting the region's rich agricultural produce, expect dishes like ratatouille, falafel, and spinach pies.

Pasta, Rice & Grains: Hearty meals that include Italian pastas like spaghetti carbonara or penne arrabbiata, and grain dishes

Breads & Pastries: Homemade bread recipes such as Italian focaccia, Turkish pide, or Moroccan flatbreads, as well as pastries like Spanish churros or Greek spanakopita.

Desserts & Sweets: Sweet endings to your meals, with recipes for treats like tiramisu, baklava, and panna cotta.

Sauces, Dips, & Spreads: Essential accompaniments like tzatziki, romesco, and tahini, which enhance the flavors of main dishes.

This cookbook contains a wealth of Mediterranean dishes waiting to be discovered and explored, so join in!

28 Day Meal Plan

Day	Breakfast	Lunch	Dinner
1	Cheesy Fig Pizzas With Garlic Oil 11	Crispy Herb Crusted Halibut 22	Mediterranean Brown Rice 66
2	Tomato And Egg Scramble 11	Picante Beef Stew 55	Veggie & Beef Ragu 66
3	Tomato And Egg Breakfast Pizza 12	Dilly Haddock In Tomato Sauce 22	Spanakopita Macaroni With Cheese 66
4	Classic Spanish Tortilla With Tuna 12	Harissa Turkey With Couscous 55	Cranberry And Almond Quinoa 67
5	Zucchini & Tomato Cheese Tart 12	Marinara Mussels 22	Turkish-style Orzo 67
6	Chocolate-strawberry Smoothie 13	Beef Stuffed Peppers 55	Rigatoni With Peppers & Mozzarella 67
7	Morning Baklava French Toast 13	Salmon & Celery Egg Bake 23	Ritzy Veggie Chili 68
8	Apple & Pumpkin Muffins 13	Chicken & Spinach Dish 56	Hearty Butternut Spinach, And Cheeses Lasagna 68
9	Scrambled Eggs With Cheese & Pancetta 14	Crispy Tilapia With Mango Salsa 23	Traditional Beef Lasagna 68
10	Tuna And Hummus Wraps 14	Slow Cooker Beef Stew 56	Baked Rolled Oat With Pears And Pecans 69
11	One-pan Tomato-basil Eggs 14	Anchovy Spread With Avocado 23	Leftover Pasta & Mushroom Frittata 69
12	Sunday Pancakes In Berry Sauce 14	Cocktail Meatballs In Almond Sauce 56	Autumn Vegetable & Rigatoni Bake 69
13	Kale-proscuitto Porridge 15	White Wine Cod Fillets 24	Pea & Mint Tortellini 70
14	Power Green Smoothie 15	Vegetable & Turkey Traybake 57	Paprika Spinach & Chickpea Bowl 70

Day	Breakfast	Lunch	Dinner
15	Skillet Eggplant & Kale Frittata 15	Vegetable & Shrimp Roast 24	Bean & Egg Noodles With Lemon Sauce 70
16	Ricotta Toast With Strawberries 16	Eggplant & Chicken Skillet 57	Easy Simple Pesto Pasta 71
17	Breakfast Pancakes With Berry Sauce 16	Roasted Salmon With Tomatoes & Capers 24	Minestrone Chickpeas And Macaroni Casserole 71
18	Fresh Mozzarella & Salmon Frittata 16	Grilled Chicken And Zucchini Kebabs 57	Cranberry & Walnut Freekeh Pilaf 71
19	Eggplant, Spinach, And Feta Sandwiches 17	Lemony Shrimp With Orzo Salad 25	Veggie & Egg Quinoa With Pancetta 72
20	Dilly Salmon Frittata 17	Creamy Chicken Balls With Almonds 58	Carrot & Barley Risotto 72
21	Chia & Almond Oatmeal 17	Instant Pot Poached Salmon 25	Kale Chicken With Pappardelle 73
22	Savory Breakfast Oatmeal 17	Easy Pork Stew 58	Quinoa With Baby Potatoes And Broccoli 73
23	Sweet Banana Pancakes With Strawberries 18	Better-for-you Cod & Potatoes 25	Friday Night Penne In Tomato Sauce 73
24	Berry & Cheese Omelet 18	Peppery Chicken Bake 58	Spanish-style Linguine With Tapenade 74
25	Spicy Tofu Tacos With Cherry Tomato Salsa 18	Shrimp & Gnocchi With Feta Cheese 26	Old-fashioned Pasta Primavera 74
26	Cayenne Tomato Oatmeal 19	Potato Lamb And Olive Stew 59	Tortellini & Cannellini With Meatballs 74
27	Anchovy & Spinach Sandwiches 19	Dill Chutney Salmon 26	Black Bean & Chickpea Burgers 75
28	Mushroom & Zucchini Egg Muffins 19	Thyme Chicken Roast 59	Spicy Bean Rolls 75

Breakfast Recipes

Cheesy Fig Pizzas With Garlic Oil

Servings:2
Cooking Time: 10 Minutes

Ingredients:

- Dough:
- 1 cup almond flour
- 1½ cups whole-wheat flour
- ¾ teaspoon instant or rapid-rise yeast
- 2 teaspoons raw honey
- 1¼ cups ice water
- 2 tablespoons extra-virgin olive oil
- 1¾ teaspoons sea salt
- Garlic Oil:
- 4 tablespoons extra-virgin olive oil, divided
- ½ teaspoon dried thyme
- 2 garlic cloves, minced
- ⅛ teaspoon sea salt
- ½ teaspoon freshly ground pepper
- Topping:
- 1 cup fresh basil leaves
- 1 cup crumbled feta cheese
- 8 ounces fresh figs, stemmed and quartered lengthwise
- 2 tablespoons raw honey

Directions:

1. Make the Dough:
2. Combine the flours, yeast, and honey in a food processor, pulse to combine well. Gently add water while pulsing. Let the dough sit for 10 minutes.
3. Mix the olive oil and salt in the dough and knead the dough until smooth. Wrap in plastic and refrigerate for at least 1 day.
4. Make the Garlic Oil:
5. Heat 2 tablespoons of olive oil in a nonstick skillet over medium-low heat until shimmering.
6. Add the thyme, garlic, salt, and pepper and sauté for 30 seconds or until fragrant. Set them aside until ready to use.
7. Make the pizzas:
8. Preheat the oven to 500ºF. Grease two baking sheets with 2 tablespoons of olive oil.
9. Divide the dough in half and shape into two balls. Press the balls into 13-inch rounds. Sprinkle the rounds with a tough of flour if they are sticky.
10. Top the rounds with the garlic oil and basil leaves, then arrange the rounds on the baking sheets. Scatter with feta cheese and figs.
11. Put the sheets in the preheated oven and bake for 9 minutes or until lightly browned. Rotate the pizza halfway through.
12. Remove the pizzas from the oven, then discard the bay leaves. Drizzle with honey. Let sit for 5 minutes and serve immediately.

Nutrition Info:

- Info Per Serving: Calories: 1350;Fat: 46.5g;Protein: 27.5g;Carbs: 221.9g.

Tomato And Egg Scramble

Servings:4
Cooking Time: 20 Minutes

Ingredients:

- 2 tablespoons extra-virgin olive oil
- ¼ cup finely minced red onion
- 1½ cups chopped fresh tomatoes
- 2 garlic cloves, minced
- ½ teaspoon dried thyme
- ½ teaspoon dried oregano
- 8 large eggs
- ½ teaspoon salt
- ¼ teaspoon freshly ground black pepper
- ¾ cup crumbled feta cheese
- ¼ cup chopped fresh mint leaves

Directions:

1. Heat the olive oil in a large skillet over medium heat.
2. Sauté the red onion and tomatoes in the hot skillet for 10 to 12 minutes, or until the tomatoes are softened.
3. Stir in the garlic, thyme, and oregano and sauté for 2 to 4 minutes, or until the garlic is fragrant.
4. Meanwhile, beat the eggs with the salt and pepper in a medium bowl until frothy.

5. Pour the beaten eggs into the skillet and reduce the heat to low. Scramble

6. for 3 to 4 minutes, stirring constantly, or until the eggs are set.

7. Remove from the heat and scatter with the feta cheese and mint. Serve warm.

Nutrition Info:

- Info Per Serving: Calories: 260;Fat: 21.9g;Protein: 10.2g;Carbs: 5.8g.

Tomato And Egg Breakfast Pizza

Servings:2
Cooking Time: 15 Minutes

Ingredients:

- 2 slices of whole-wheat naan bread
- 2 tablespoons prepared pesto
- 1 medium tomato, sliced
- 2 large eggs

Directions:

1. Heat a large nonstick skillet over medium-high heat. Place the naan bread in the skillet and let warm for about 2 minutes on each side, or until softened.
2. Spread 1 tablespoon of the pesto on one side of each slice and top with tomato slices.
3. Remove from the skillet and place each one on its own plate.
4. Crack the eggs into the skillet, keeping them separated, and cook until the whites are no longer translucent and the yolk is cooked to desired doneness.
5. Using a spatula, spoon one egg onto each bread slice. Serve warm.

Nutrition Info:

- Info Per Serving: Calories: 429;Fat: 16.8g;Protein: 18.1g;Carbs: 12.0g.

Classic Spanish Tortilla With Tuna

Servings:4
Cooking Time:30 Minutes

Ingredients:

- 7 oz canned tuna packed in water, flaked
- 2 plum tomatoes, seeded and diced
- 2 tbsp olive oil
- 6 large eggs, beaten
- 2 small potatoes, diced
- 2 green onions, chopped
- 1 roasted red bell pepper, sliced
- 1 tsp dried tarragon

Directions:

1. Preheat your broiler to high. Heat the olive oil in a skillet over medium heat. Fry the potatoes for 7 minutes until slightly soft. Add the green onions and cook for 3 minutes. Stir in the tuna, tomatoes, peppers, tarragon, and eggs. Cook for 8-10 minutes until the eggs are bubbling from the bottom and the bottom is slightly brown. Place the skillet under the preheated broiler for 5-6 minutes or until the middle is set and the top is slightly brown. Serve sliced into wedges.

Nutrition Info:

- Info Per Serving: Calories: 422;Fat: 21g;Protein: 14g;Carbs: 46g.

Zucchini & Tomato Cheese Tart

Servings:6
Cooking Time:60 Minutes

Ingredients:

- 3 tbsp olive oil
- 5 sun-dried tomatoes, chopped
- 1 prepared pie crust
- 1 onion, chopped
- 2 garlic cloves, minced
- 2 zucchinis, chopped
- 1 red bell pepper, chopped
- 6 Kalamata olives, sliced
- 1 tsp fresh dill, chopped
- ½ cup Greek yogurt
- 1 cup feta cheese, crumbled
- 4 eggs
- 1 ½ cups milk
- Salt and black pepper to taste

Directions:

1. Preheat the oven to 380 F. Warm the olive oil in a skillet over medium heat and sauté garlic and onion for 3 minutes. Add in bell pepper and zucchini and sauté for another 3 minutes. Stir in olives, dill, salt, and pepper for 1-2 minutes and add tomatoes and feta cheese. Mix well and turn the heat off.
2. Press the crust gently into a lightly greased pie dish and prick it with a fork. Bake in the oven for 10-15 minutes until pale gold. Spread the zucchini mixture over the pie crust. Whisk the eggs with salt, pepper, milk, and yogurt in a bowl, then pour over the zucchini layer. Bake for 25-30 minutes until golden brown. Let cool before serving.

Nutrition Info:

- Info Per Serving: Calories: 220;Fat: 16g;Protein: 10g;Carbs: 14g.

Chocolate-strawberry Smoothie

Servings:2
Cooking Time:5 Minutes

Ingredients:

- 1 cup buttermilk
- 2 cups strawberries, hulled
- 1 cup crushed ice
- 3 tbsp cocoa powder
- 3 tbsp honey
- 2 mint leaves

Directions:

1. In a food processor, pulse buttermilk, strawberries, ice, cocoa powder, mint, and honey until smooth. Serve.

Nutrition Info:

- Info Per Serving: Calories: 209;Fat: 2.6g;Protein: 7g;Carbs: 47.2g.

Morning Baklava French Toast

Servings:2
Cooking Time:20 Minutes

Ingredients:

- 2 tbsp orange juice
- 3 fresh eggs, beaten
- 1 tsp lemon zest
- 1/8 tsp vanilla extract
- ¼ cup honey
- 2 tbsp whole milk
- ¾ tsp ground cinnamon
- ¼ cup walnuts, crumbled
- ¼ cup pistachios, crumbled
- 1 tbsp sugar
- 2 tbsp white bread crumbs
- 4 slices bread
- 2 tbsp unsalted butter
- 1 tsp confectioners' sugar

Directions:

1. Combine the eggs, orange juice, lemon zest, vanilla, honey, milk, and cinnamon in a bowl; set aside. Pulse walnuts and pistachios in a food processor until they are finely crumbled. In a small bowl, mix the walnuts, pistachios, sugar, and bread crumbs. Spread the nut mixture on 2 bread slices.
2. Cover with the remaining 2 slices. Melt the butter in a skillet over medium heat. Dip the sandwiches into the egg mixture and fry them for 4 minutes on both sides or until golden. Remove to a plate and cut them diagonally. Dust with confectioners' sugar. Serve immediately.

Nutrition Info:

- Info Per Serving: Calories: 651;Fat: 30g;Protein: 21g;Carbs: 80g.

Apple & Pumpkin Muffins

Servings:12
Cooking Time:30 Minutes

Ingredients:

- ½ cup butter, melted
- 1 ½ cups granulated sugar
- ½ cup sugar
- ¾ cup flour
- 2 tsp pumpkin pie spice
- 1 tsp baking soda
- ¼ tsp salt
- ¼ tsp nutmeg
- 1 apple, grated
- 1 can pumpkin puree
- ½ cup full-fat yogurt
- 2 large egg whites

Directions:

1. Preheat the oven to 350 F. In a bowl, mix sugars, flour, pumpkin pie spice, baking soda, salt, and nutmeg. In a separate bowl, mix apple, pumpkin puree, yogurt, and butter.
2. Slowly mix the wet ingredients into the dry ingredients. Using a mixer on high, whip the egg whites until stiff and fold them into the batter. Pour the batter into a greased muffin tin, filling each cup halfway. Bake for 25 minutes or until a fork inserted in the center comes out clean. Let cool.

Nutrition Info:

- Info Per Serving: Calories: 259;Fat: 8.2g;Protein: 3g;Carbs: 49.1g.

Scrambled Eggs With Cheese & Pancetta

Servings:4
Cooking Time:1 Hour 15 Minutes

Ingredients:

- 2 tbsp olive oil
- 4 eggs, whisked
- 1 red onion, chopped
- 3 oz pancetta, chopped
- 2 garlic cloves, minced
- 2 oz goat cheese, crumbled
- 1 tbsp basil, chopped
- Salt and black pepper to taste

Directions:

1. Warm half of oil in a skillet over medium heat and sauté onion, pancetta, and garlic for 3 minutes. Add in goat cheese and whisked eggs and cook for 5-6 minutes, stirring often. Season with salt and pepper. Sprinkle with basil and serve.

Nutrition Info:

- Info Per Serving: Calories: 315;Fat: 25.3g;Protein: 18g;Carbs: 4g.

Tuna And Hummus Wraps

Servings:2
Cooking Time: 0 Minutes

Ingredients:

- Hummus:
- 1 cup from 1 can low-sodium chickpeas, drained and rinsed
- 2 tablespoons tahini
- 1 tablespoon extra-virgin olive oil
- 1 garlic clove
- Juice of ½ lemon
- ¼ teaspoon salt
- 2 tablespoons water
- Wraps:
- 4 large lettuce leaves
- 1 can chunk light tuna packed in water, drained
- 1 red bell pepper, seeded and cut into strips
- 1 cucumber, sliced

Directions:

1. Make the Hummus
2. In a blender jar, combine the chickpeas, tahini, olive oil, garlic, lemon juice, salt, and water. Process until smooth. Taste and adjust with additional lemon juice or salt, as needed.
3. Make the Wraps
4. On each lettuce leaf, spread 1 tablespoon of hummus, and divide the tuna among the leaves. Top each with several strips of red pepper and cucumber slices.
5. Roll up the lettuce leaves, folding in the two shorter sides and rolling away from you, like a burrito. Serve immediately.

Nutrition Info:

- Info Per Serving: Calories: 192;Fat: 5.1g;Protein: 26.1g;Carbs: 15.1g.

One-pan Tomato-basil Eggs

Servings:2
Cooking Time:25 Minutes

Ingredients:

- 2 tsp olive oil
- 2 eggs, whisked
- 2 tomatoes, cubed
- 1 tbsp basil, chopped
- 1 green onion, chopped
- Salt and black pepper to taste

Directions:

1. Warm the oil in a skillet over medium heat and sauté tomatoes, green onion, salt, and pepper for 5 minutes. Stir in eggs and cook for another 10 minutes. Serve topped with basil.

Nutrition Info:

- Info Per Serving: Calories: 310;Fat: 15g;Protein: 12g;Carbs: 18g.

Sunday Pancakes In Berry Sauce

Servings:4
Cooking Time:20 Minutes

Ingredients:

- Pancakes
- 6 tbsp olive oil
- 1 cup flour
- 1 tsp baking powder
- ¼ tsp salt
- 2 large eggs
- 1 lemon, zested and juiced
- ½ tsp vanilla extract
- ½ tsp dark rum
- Berry Sauce

- 1 cup mixed berries
- 3 tbsp sugar
- 1 tbsp lemon juice
- ½ tsp vanilla extract

Directions:

1. In a large bowl, combine the flour, baking powder, and salt and whisk to break up any clumps. Add 4 tablespoons of olive oil, eggs, lemon zest and juice, rum, and vanilla extract and whisk to combine well. Brush a frying pan with butter over medium heat and cook the pancakes for 5-7 minutes, flipping once until bubbles begin to form.
2. To make the sauce, pour the mixed berries, lemon juice, vanilla, and sugar in a small saucepan over medium heat. Cook for 3-4 minutes until bubbly, adding a little water if the mixture is too thick. Mash the berries with a fork and stir until smooth. Pour over the pancakes and serve.

Nutrition Info:

- Info Per Serving: Calories: 275;Fat: 26g;Protein: 4g;Carbs: 8g.

Kale-proscuitto Porridge

Servings:2
Cooking Time:30 Minutes

Ingredients:

- 1 tbsp olive oil
- 1 green onion, chopped
- 1 oz prosciutto, chopped
- 2 cups kale
- ¾ cup old-fashioned oats
- 2 tbsp Parmesan, grated
- Salt and black pepper to taste

Directions:

1. Warm the olive oil in a pan over medium heat. Sauté the onion and prosciutto and sauté for 4 minutes or until the prosciutto is crisp and the onion turns golden. Add the kale and stir for 5 minutes until wilted. Transfer to a bowl.
2. Add the oats to the pan and let them toast for 2 minutes. Add 1 ½ of water or chicken stock and bring to a boil. Reduce the heat to low, cover, and let the oats simmer for 10 minutes or until the liquid is absorbed and the oats are tender.
3. Stir in Parmesan cheese, and add the onions, prosciutto, and kale back to the pan and cook until creamy but not dry. Adjust the seasoning with salt and pepper and serve.

Nutrition Info:

- Info Per Serving: Calories: 258;Fat: 12g;Protein: 11g;Carbs: 29g.

Power Green Smoothie

Servings:1
Cooking Time:10 Minutes

Ingredients:

- 1 tbsp extra-virgin olive oil
- 1 avocado, peeled and pitted
- 1 cup milk
- ½ cup watercress
- ½ cup baby spinach leaves
- ½ cucumber, peeled and seeded
- 10 mint leaves, stems removed
- ½ lemon, juiced

Directions:

1. In a blender, mix avocado, milk, baby spinach, watercress, cucumber, olive oil, mint, and lemon juice and blend until smooth and creamy. Add more milk or water to achieve your desired consistency. Serve chilled or at room temperature.

Nutrition Info:

- Info Per Serving: Calories: 330;Fat: 30.2g;Protein: 4g;Carbs: 19g.

Skillet Eggplant & Kale Frittata

Servings:1
Cooking Time:20 Minutes

Ingredients:

- 1 tbsp olive oil
- 3 large eggs
- 1 tsp milk
- 1 cup curly kale, torn
- ½ eggplant, peeled and diced
- ¼ red bell pepper, chopped
- Salt and black pepper to taste
- 1 oz crumbled Goat cheese

Directions:

1. Preheat your broiler. Whisk the eggs with milk, salt, and pepper until just combined. Heat the olive oil in a small skillet over medium heat. Spread the eggs on the bottom and add the kale on top in an even layer; top with veggies.

2. Season with salt and pepper. Allow the eggs and vegetables to cook 3 to 5 minutes until the bottom half of the eggs are firm and vegetables are tender. Top with the crumbled Goat cheese and place under the broiler for 5 minutes until the eggs are firm in the middle and the cheese has melted. Slice into wedges and serve immediately.

Nutrition Info:

- Info Per Serving: Calories: 622;Fat: 39g;Protein: 41g;Carbs: 33g.

Ricotta Toast With Strawberries

Servings:2
Cooking Time: 0 Minutes

Ingredients:

- ½ cup crumbled ricotta cheese
- 1 tablespoon honey, plus additional as needed
- Pinch of sea salt, plus additional as needed
- 4 slices of whole-grain bread, toasted
- 1 cup sliced fresh strawberries
- 4 large fresh basil leaves, sliced into thin shreds

Directions:

1. Mix together the cheese, honey, and salt in a small bowl until well incorporated.
2. Taste and add additional salt and honey if needed.
3. Spoon 2 tablespoons of the cheese mixture onto each slice of bread and spread it all over.
4. Sprinkle the sliced strawberry and basil leaves on top before serving.

Nutrition Info:

- Info Per Serving: Calories: 274;Fat: 7.9g;Protein: 15.1g;Carbs: 39.8g.

Breakfast Pancakes With Berry Sauce

Servings:4
Cooking Time: 10 Minutes

Ingredients:

- Pancakes:
- 1 cup almond flour
- 1 teaspoon baking powder
- ¼ teaspoon salt
- 6 tablespoon extra-virgin olive oil, divided
- 2 large eggs, beaten
- Zest and juice of 1 lemon
- ½ teaspoon vanilla extract
- Berry Sauce:
- 1 cup frozen mixed berries
- 1 tablespoon water, plus more as needed
- ½ teaspoon vanilla extract

Directions:

1. Make the Pancakes
2. In a large bowl, combine the almond flour, baking powder, and salt and stir to break up any clumps.
3. Add 4 tablespoons olive oil, beaten eggs, lemon zest and juice, and vanilla extract and stir until well mixed.
4. Heat 1 tablespoon of olive oil in a large skillet. Spoon about 2 tablespoons of batter for each pancake. Cook until bubbles begin to form, 4 to 5 minutes. Flip and cook for another 2 to 3 minutes. Repeat with the remaining 1 tablespoon of olive oil and batter.
5. Make the Berry Sauce
6. Combine the frozen berries, water, and vanilla extract in a small saucepan and heat over medium-high heat for 3 to 4 minutes until bubbly, adding more water as needed. Using the back of a spoon or fork, mash the berries and whisk until smooth.
7. Serve the pancakes with the berry sauce.

Nutrition Info:

- Info Per Serving: Calories: 275;Fat: 26.0g;Protein: 4.0g;Carbs: 8.0g.

Fresh Mozzarella & Salmon Frittata

Servings:4
Cooking Time:15 Minutes

Ingredients:

- 1 ball fresh mozzarella cheese, chopped
- 2 tsp olive oil
- 8 fresh eggs
- ½ cup whole milk
- 1 spring onion, chopped
- ¼ cup chopped fresh basil
- Salt and black pepper to taste
- 3 oz smoked salmon, chopped

Directions:

1. Preheat your broiler to medium. Whisk the eggs with milk, spring onion, basil, pepper, and salt in a bowl. Heat the olive oil in a skillet over medium heat and pour in the egg mixture.
2. Top with mozzarella cheese and cook for 3–5 minutes until the frittata is set on the bottom and the egg is almost set but still moist on top. Scatter over the salmon and place the skillet under the preheated broiler for

1-2 minutes or until set and slightly puffed. Cut the frittata into wedges. Enjoy!

Nutrition Info:

- Info Per Serving: Calories: 351;Fat: 13g;Protein: 52g;Carbs: 6g.

Eggplant, Spinach, And Feta Sandwiches

Servings:2
Cooking Time: 6 To 8 Minutes

Ingredients:

- 1 medium eggplant, sliced into ½-inch-thick slices
- 2 tablespoons olive oil
- Sea salt and freshly ground pepper, to taste
- 5 to 6 tablespoons hummus
- 4 slices whole-wheat bread, toasted
- 1 cup baby spinach leaves
- 2 ounces feta cheese, softened

Directions:

1. Preheat the grill to medium-high heat.
2. Salt both sides of the sliced eggplant, and let sit for 20 minutes to draw out the bitter juices.
3. Rinse the eggplant and pat dry with a paper towel.
4. Brush the eggplant slices with olive oil and season with sea salt and freshly ground pepper to taste.
5. Grill the eggplant until lightly charred on both sides but still slightly firm in the middle, about 3 to 4 minutes per side.
6. Spread the hummus on the bread slices and top with the spinach leaves, feta cheese, and grilled eggplant. Top with the other slice of bread and serve immediately.

Nutrition Info:

- Info Per Serving: Calories: 493;Fat: 25.3g;Protein: 17.1g;Carbs: 50.9g.

Dilly Salmon Frittata

Servings:4
Cooking Time:35 Minutes

Ingredients:

- 2 tbsp olive oil
- 1 cup cream cheese
- 1 cup smoked salmon, chopped
- 8 eggs, whisked
- 1 tsp dill, chopped
- 2 tbsp milk
- Salt and black pepper to taste

Directions:

1. Preheat oven to 360 F. In a bowl, place all the ingredients and stir to combine. Warm olive oil in a pan over medium heat and pour in the mixture. Cook until the base is set, about 3-4 minutes. Place the pan in the oven and bake until the top is golden, about 5 minutes. Serve sliced into wedges.

Nutrition Info:

- Info Per Serving: Calories: 418;Fat: 37g;Protein: 19.6g;Carbs: 3g.

Chia & Almond Oatmeal

Servings:2
Cooking Time:10 Min + Chilling Time

Ingredients:

- ¼ tsp almond extract
- ½ cup milk
- ½ cup rolled oats
- 2 tbsp almonds, sliced
- 2 tbsp sugar
- 1 tsp chia seeds
- ¼ tsp ground cardamom
- ¼ tsp ground cinnamon

Directions:

1. Combine the milk, oats, almonds, sugar, chia seeds, cardamom, almond extract, and cinnamon in a mason jar and shake well. Keep in the refrigerator for 4 hours. Serve.

Nutrition Info:

- Info Per Serving: Calories: 131;Fat: 6.2g;Protein: 4.9g;Carbs: 17g.

Savory Breakfast Oatmeal

Servings:2
Cooking Time: 15 Minutes

Ingredients:

- ½ cup steel-cut oats
- 1 cup water
- 1 medium cucumber, chopped
- 1 large tomato, chopped
- 1 tablespoon olive oil
- Pinch freshly grated Parmesan cheese
- Sea salt and freshly ground pepper, to taste

- Flat-leaf parsley or mint, chopped, for garnish

Directions:

1. Combine the oats and water in a medium saucepan and bring to a boil over high heat, stirring continuously, or until the water is absorbed, about 15 minutes.
2. Divide the oatmeal between 2 bowls and scatter the tomato and cucumber on top. Drizzle with the olive oil and sprinkle with the Parmesan cheese.
3. Season with salt and pepper to taste. Serve garnished with the parsley.

Nutrition Info:

- Info Per Serving: Calories: 197;Fat: 8.9g;Protein: 6.3g;Carbs: 23.1g.

Sweet Banana Pancakes With Strawberries

Servings:4
Cooking Time:15 Minutes

Ingredients:

- 2 tbsp olive oil
- 1 cup flour
- 1 cup + 2 tbsp milk
- 2 eggs, beaten
- ⅓ cup honey
- 1 tsp baking soda
- ¼ tsp salt
- 1 sliced banana
- 1 cup sliced strawberries
- 1 tbsp maple syrup

Directions:

1. Mix together the flour, milk, eggs, honey, baking soda, and salt in a bowl. Warm the olive oil in a skillet over medium heat and pour in ⅓ cup of the pancake batter. Cook for 2-3 minutes. Add half of the fresh fruit and flip to cook for 2-3 minutes on the other side until cooked through. Top with the remaining fruit, drizzle with maple syrup and serve.

Nutrition Info:

- Info Per Serving: Calories: 415;Fat: 24g;Protein: 12g;Carbs: 46g.

Berry & Cheese Omelet

Servings:4
Cooking Time:10 Minutes

Ingredients:

- 2 tbsp olive oil
- 6 eggs, whisked
- 1 tsp cinnamon powder
- 1 cup ricotta cheese
- 4 oz berries

Directions:

1. Whisk eggs, cinnamon powder, ricotta cheese, and berries in a bowl. Warm the olive oil in a skillet over medium heat and pour in the egg mixture. Cook for 2 minutes, turn the egg and cook for 2 minutes more. Serve immediately.

Nutrition Info:

- Info Per Serving: Calories: 256;Fat: 18g;Protein: 15.6g;Carbs: 7g.

Spicy Tofu Tacos With Cherry Tomato Salsa

Servings:4
Cooking Time: 11 Minutes

Ingredients:

- Cherry Tomato Salsa:
- ¼ cup sliced cherry tomatoes
- ½ jalapeño, deseeded and sliced
- Juice of 1 lime
- 1 garlic clove, minced
- Sea salt and freshly ground black pepper, to taste
- 2 teaspoons extra-virgin olive oil
- Spicy Tofu Taco Filling:
- 4 tablespoons water, divided
- ½ cup canned black beans, rinsed and drained
- 2 teaspoons fresh chopped chives, divided
- ¾ teaspoon ground cumin, divided
- ¾ teaspoon smoked paprika, divided
- Dash cayenne pepper (optional)
- ¼ teaspoon sea salt
- ¼ teaspoon freshly ground black pepper
- 1 teaspoon extra-virgin olive oil
- 6 ounces firm tofu, drained, rinsed, and pressed
- 4 corn tortillas
- ¼ avocado, sliced
- ¼ cup fresh cilantro

Directions:

1. Make the Cherry Tomato Salsa:
2. Combine the ingredients for the salsa in a small bowl. Stir to mix well. Set aside until ready to use.
3. Make the Spicy Tofu Taco Filling:
4. Add 2 tablespoons of water into a saucepan, then add the black beans and sprinkle with 1 teaspoon of chives, ½ teaspoon of cumin, ¼ teaspoon of smoked paprika, and cayenne. Stir to mix well.
5. Cook for 5 minutes over medium heat until heated through, then mash the black beans with the back of a spoon. Turn off the heat and set aside.
6. Add remaining water into a bowl, then add the remaining chives, cumin, and paprika. Sprinkle with cayenne, salt, and black pepper. Stir to mix well. Set aside.
7. Heat the olive oil in a nonstick skillet over medium heat until shimmering.
8. Add the tofu and drizzle with taco sauce, then sauté for 5 minutes or until the seasoning is absorbed. Remove the tofu from the skillet and set aside.
9. Warm the tortillas in the skillet for 1 minutes or until heated through.
10. Transfer the tortillas onto a large plate and top with tofu, mashed black beans, avocado, cilantro, then drizzle the tomato salsa over. Serve immediately.

Nutrition Info:

- Info Per Serving: Calories: 240;Fat: 9.0g;Protein: 11.6g;Carbs: 31.6g.

Cayenne Tomato Oatmeal

Servings:4
Cooking Time:35 Minutes

Ingredients:

- 1 tbsp olive oil
- 1 cup milk
- 3 cups water
- 1 cup steel-cut oats
- 10 cherry tomatoes, halved
- 1 tsp cayenne pepper

Directions:

1. Combine milk and 3 cups of water in a saucepan over medium heat and bring to a boil. Warm the olive oil in a skillet over medium heat and sauté oats for 2 minutes.
2. Remove into the milk saucepan. Mix in oats and cherry tomatoes and simmer for 23 minutes over medium heat. Serve in bowls sprinkled with cayenne pepper and serve.

Nutrition Info:

- Info Per Serving: Calories: 180;Fat: 20g;Protein: 2g;Carbs: 4g.

Anchovy & Spinach Sandwiches

Servings:2
Cooking Time:5 Minutes

Ingredients:

- 1 avocado, mashed
- 4 anchovies, drained
- 4 whole-wheat bread slices
- 1 cup baby spinach
- 1 tomato, sliced

Directions:

1. Spread the slices of bread with avocado mash and arrange the anchovies over. Top with baby spinach and tomato slices.

Nutrition Info:

- Info Per Serving: Calories: 300;Fat: 12g;Protein: 5g;Carbs: 10g.

Mushroom & Zucchini Egg Muffins

Servings:4
Cooking Time:20 Minutes

Ingredients:

- 2 tbsp olive oil
- 1 cup Parmesan, grated
- 1 onion, chopped
- 1 cup mushrooms, sliced
- 1 red bell pepper, chopped
- 1 zucchini, chopped
- Salt and black pepper to taste
- 8 eggs, whisked
- 2 tbsp chives, chopped

Directions:

1. Preheat the oven to 360 F. Warm the olive oil in a skillet over medium heat and sauté onion, bell pepper, zucchini, mushrooms, salt, and pepper for 5 minutes until tender. Mix with eggs and season with salt and pepper. Distribute the mixture across muffin cups and top with the Parmesan cheese. Sprinkle with chives and bake for 10 minutes. Serve.

Nutrition Info:

- Info Per Serving: Calories: 60;Fat: 4g;Protein: 5g;-Carbs: 4g.

Mediterranean Eggs (shakshuka)

Servings:4
Cooking Time: 20 Minutes

Ingredients:

- 2 tablespoons extra-virgin olive oil
- 1 cup chopped shallots
- 1 teaspoon garlic powder
- 1 cup finely diced potato
- 1 cup chopped red bell peppers
- 1 can diced tomatoes, drained
- ¼ teaspoon ground cardamom
- ¼ teaspoon paprika
- ¼ teaspoon turmeric
- 4 large eggs
- ¼ cup chopped fresh cilantro

Directions:

1. Preheat the oven to 350ºF.
2. Heat the olive oil in an ovenproof skillet over medium-high heat until it shimmers.
3. Add the shallots and sauté for about 3 minutes, stirring occasionally, until fragrant.
4. Fold in the garlic powder, potato, and bell peppers and stir to combine.
5. Cover and cook for 10 minutes, stirring frequently.
6. Add the tomatoes, cardamon, paprika, and turmeric and mix well.
7. When the mixture begins to bubble, remove from the heat and crack the eggs into the skillet.
8. Transfer the skillet to the preheated oven and bake for 5 to 10 minutes, or until the egg whites are set and the yolks are cooked to your liking.
9. Remove from the oven and garnish with the cilantro before serving.

Nutrition Info:

- Info Per Serving: Calories: 223;Fat: 11.8g;Protein: 9.1g;Carbs: 19.5g.

Brown Rice And Black Bean Burgers

Servings:8
Cooking Time: 40 Minutes

Ingredients:

- 1 cup cooked brown rice
- 1 can black beans, drained and rinsed
- 1 tablespoon olive oil
- 2 tablespoons taco or seasoning
- ½ yellow onion, finely diced
- 1 beet, peeled and grated
- 1 carrot, peeled and grated
- 2 tablespoons no-salt-added tomato paste
- 2 tablespoons apple cider vinegar
- 3 garlic cloves, minced
- ¼ teaspoon sea salt
- Ground black pepper, to taste
- 8 whole-wheat hamburger buns
- Toppings:
- 16 lettuce leaves, rinsed well
- 8 tomato slices, rinsed well
- Whole-grain mustard, to taste

Directions:

1. Line a baking sheet with parchment paper.
2. Put the brown rice and black beans in a food processor and pulse until mix well. Pour the mixture in a large bowl and set aside.
3. Heat the olive oil in a nonstick skillet over medium heat until shimmering.
4. Add the taco seasoning and stir for 1 minute or until fragrant.
5. Add the onion, beet, and carrot and sauté for 5 minutes or until the onion is translucent and beet and carrot are tender.
6. Pour in the tomato paste and vinegar, then add the garlic and cook for 3 minutes or until the sauce is thickened. Sprinkle with salt and ground black pepper.
7. Transfer the vegetable mixture to the bowl of rice mixture, then stir to mix well until smooth.
8. Divide and shape the mixture into 8 patties, then arrange the patties on the baking sheet and refrigerate for at least 1 hour.
9. Preheat the oven to 400ºF.
10. Remove the baking sheet from the refrigerator and allow to sit under room temperature for 10 minutes.
11. Bake in the preheated oven for 40 minutes or until golden brown on both sides. Flip the patties halfway through the cooking time.
12. Remove the patties from the oven and allow to cool for 10 minutes.
13. Assemble the buns with patties, lettuce, and tomato slices. Top the filling with mustard and serve immediately.

Nutrition Info:

- Info Per Serving: Calories: 544;Fat: 20.0g;Protein: 15.8g;Carbs: 76.0g.

Fish And Seafood Recipes

Crispy Herb Crusted Halibut

Servings:4
Cooking Time: 20 Minutes

Ingredients:

- 4 halibut fillets, patted dry
- Extra-virgin olive oil, for brushing
- ½ cup coarsely ground unsalted pistachios
- 1 tablespoon chopped fresh parsley
- 1 teaspoon chopped fresh basil
- 1 teaspoon chopped fresh thyme
- Pinch sea salt
- Pinch freshly ground black pepper

Directions:

1. Preheat the oven to 350ºF. Line a baking sheet with parchment paper.
2. Place the fillets on the baking sheet and brush them generously with olive oil.
3. In a small bowl, stir together the pistachios, parsley, basil, thyme, salt, and pepper.
4. Spoon the nut mixture evenly on the fish, spreading it out so the tops of the fillets are covered.
5. Bake in the preheated oven until it flakes when pressed with a fork, about 20 minutes.
6. Serve immediately.

Nutrition Info:

- Info Per Serving: Calories: 262;Fat: 11.0g;Protein: 32.0g;Carbs: 4.0g.

Dilly Haddock In Tomato Sauce

Servings:4
Cooking Time:20 Minutes

Ingredients:

- 4 haddock fillets, boneless
- 1 cup vegetable stock
- 2 garlic cloves, minced
- 2 cups cherry tomatoes, halved
- Salt and black pepper to taste
- 2 tbsp dill, chopped

Directions:

1. In a skillet over medium heat, cook cherry tomatoes, garlic, salt, and pepper for 5 minutes. Stir in haddock fillets and vegetable stock and bring to a simmer. Cook covered for 10-12 minutes. Serve topped with dill.

Nutrition Info:

- Info Per Serving: Calories: 190;Fat: 2g;Protein: 35g;Carbs: 6g.

Marinara Mussels

Servings:4
Cooking Time:25 Minutes

Ingredients:

- 2 lb mussels, cleaned and de-bearded
- 2 tbsp olive oil
- 2 leeks, chopped
- 1 red onion, chopped
- Salt and black pepper to taste
- 1 tbsp parsley, chopped
- 1 tbsp chives, chopped
- ½ cup tomato sauce

Directions:

1. Warm the olive oil in a skillet over medium heat and cook leeks and onion for 5 minutes. Stir in mussels, salt, pepper, parsley, chives, and tomato sauce and cook for 10 minutes. Discard any unopened mussels. Serve right away.

Nutrition Info:

- Info Per Serving: Calories: 250;Fat: 10g;Protein: 9g;Carbs: 16g.

Salmon & Celery Egg Bake

Servings:4
Cooking Time:40 Minutes

Ingredients:

- 2 tbsp olive oil
- 2 tbsp butter, melted
- 4 oz smoked salmon, flaked
- 1 cup cheddar cheese, grated
- 4 eggs, whisked
- ¼ cup plain yogurt
- 1 cup cream of celery soup
- 1 shallot, chopped
- 2 garlic cloves, minced
- ½ cup celery, chopped
- 8 slices fresh toast, cubed
- 1 tbsp mint leaves, chopped

Directions:

1. Preheat the oven to 360 F. In a bowl, mix eggs, yogurt, and celery soup. Warm olive oil in a skillet over medium heat and cook the shallot, garlic, and celery until tender. Place the toast cubes in a greased baking dish, top with cooked vegetables and salmon, and cover with egg mixture and butter. Bake for 22-25 minutes until it is cooked through. Scatter cheddar cheese on top and bake for another 5 minutes until the cheese melts. Serve garnished with mint leaves.

Nutrition Info:

- Info Per Serving: Calories: 392;Fat: 31g;Protein: 20g;Carbs: 9.6g.

Crispy Tilapia With Mango Salsa

Servings:2
Cooking Time: 10 Minutes

Ingredients:

- Salsa:
- 1 cup chopped mango
- 2 tablespoons chopped fresh cilantro
- 2 tablespoons chopped red onion
- 2 tablespoons freshly squeezed lime juice
- ½ jalapeño pepper, seeded and minced
- Pinch salt
- Tilapia:
- 1 tablespoon paprika
- 1 teaspoon onion powder
- ½ teaspoon dried thyme
- ½ teaspoon freshly ground black pepper
- ¼ teaspoon cayenne pepper
- ½ teaspoon garlic powder
- ¼ teaspoon salt
- ½ pound boneless tilapia fillets
- 2 teaspoons extra-virgin olive oil
- 1 lime, cut into wedges, for serving

Directions:

1. Make the salsa: Place the mango, cilantro, onion, lime juice, jalapeño, and salt in a medium bowl and toss to combine. Set aside.
2. Make the tilapia: Stir together the paprika, onion powder, thyme, black pepper, cayenne pepper, garlic powder, and salt in a small bowl until well mixed. Rub both sides of fillets generously with the mixture.
3. Heat the olive oil in a large skillet over medium heat.
4. Add the fish fillets and cook each side for 3 to 5 minutes until golden brown and cooked through.
5. Divide the fillets among two plates and spoon half of the prepared salsa onto each fillet. Serve the fish alongside the lime wedges.

Nutrition Info:

- Info Per Serving: Calories: 239;Fat: 7.8g;Protein: 25.0g;Carbs: 21.9g.

Anchovy Spread With Avocado

Servings:2
Cooking Time:5 Minutes

Ingredients:

- 1 avocado, peeled and pitted
- 1 tsp lemon juice
- ¼ celery stalk, chopped
- ¼ cup chopped shallots
- 2 anchovy fillets in olive oil
- Salt and black pepper to taste

Directions:

1. Combine lemon juice, avocado, celery, shallots, and anchovy fillets (with their olive oil) in a food processor. Blitz until smooth. Season with salt and black pepper. Serve.

Nutrition Info:

- Info Per Serving: Calories: 271;Fat: 20g;Protein: 15g;Carbs: 12g.

White Wine Cod Fillets

Servings:4
Cooking Time:40 Minutes

Ingredients:

- 4 cod fillets
- Salt and black pepper to taste
- ½ fennel seeds, ground
- 1 tbsp olive oil
- ½ cup dry white wine
- ½ cup vegetable stock
- 2 garlic cloves, minced
- 1 tsp chopped fresh sage
- 4 rosemary sprigs

Directions:

1. Preheat oven to 375 F. Season the cod fillets with salt, pepper, and ground fennel seeds and place them in a greased baking dish. Add the wine, stock, garlic, and sage and drizzle with olive oil. Cover with foil and bake for 20 minutes until the fish flakes easily with a fork. Remove the fillets from the dish. Place the liquid in a saucepan over high heat and cook, stirring frequently, until reduced by half, about 10 minutes. Serve the fish topped with sauce and fresh rosemary sprigs.

Nutrition Info:

- Info Per Serving: Calories: 89;Fat: 0.6g;Protein: 18g;Carbs: 1.8g.

Vegetable & Shrimp Roast

Servings:4
Cooking Time:30 Minutes

Ingredients:

- 2 lb shrimp, peeled and deveined
- 4 tbsp olive oil
- 2 bell peppers, cut into chunks
- 2 fennel bulbs, cut into wedges
- 2 red onions, cut into wedges
- 4 garlic cloves, unpeeled
- 8 Kalamata olives, halved
- 1 tsp lemon zest, grated
- 2 tsp oregano, dried
- 2 tbsp parsley, chopped
- Salt and black pepper to taste

Directions:

1. Preheat the oven to 390 F. Place bell peppers, garlic, fennel, red onions, and olives in a roasting tray. Add in the lemon zest, oregano, half of the olive oil, salt, and pepper and toss to coat; roast for 15 minutes. Coat the shrimp with the remaining olive oil and pour over the veggies; roast for another 7 minutes. Serve topped with parsley.

Nutrition Info:

- Info Per Serving: Calories: 350;Fat: 20g;Protein: 11g;Carbs: 35g.

Roasted Salmon With Tomatoes & Capers

Servings:4
Cooking Time:25 Minutes

Ingredients:

- 1 tbsp olive oil
- 4 salmon steaks
- Salt and black pepper to taste
- ¼ mustard powder
- ½ tsp garlic powder
- 2 Roma tomatoes, chopped
- ¼ cup green olives, chopped
- 1 tsp capers
- ½ cup breadcrumbs
- 1 lemon, cut into wedges

Directions:

1. Preheat oven to 375 F. Arrange the salmon fillets on a greased baking dish. Season with salt, pepper, garlic powder, and mustard powder and coat with the breadcrumbs. Drizzle with olive oil. Scatter the tomatoes, green olives, garlic, and capers around the fish fillets. Bake for 15 minutes until the salmon steaks flake easily with a fork. Serve with lemon wedges.

Nutrition Info:

- Info Per Serving: Calories: 504;Fat: 18g;Protein: 68g;Carbs: 14g.

Lemony Shrimp With Orzo Salad

Servings:4
Cooking Time: 22 Minutes

Ingredients:

- 1 cup orzo
- 1 hothouse cucumber, deseeded and chopped
- ½ cup finely diced red onion
- 2 tablespoons extra-virgin olive oil
- 2 pounds shrimp, peeled and deveined
- 3 lemons, juiced
- Salt and freshly ground black pepper, to taste
- ¾ cup crumbled feta cheese
- 2 tablespoons dried dill
- 1 cup chopped fresh flat-leaf parsley

Directions:

1. Bring a large pot of water to a boil. Add the orzo and cook covered for 15 to 18 minutes, or until the orzo is tender. Transfer to a colander to drain and set aside to cool.
2. Mix the cucumber and red onion in a bowl. Set aside.
3. Heat the olive oil in a medium skillet over medium heat until it shimmers.
4. Reduce the heat, add the shrimp, and cook each side for 2 minutes until cooked through.
5. Add the cooked shrimp to the bowl of cucumber and red onion. Mix in the cooked orzo and lemon juice and toss to combine. Sprinkle with salt and pepper. Scatter the top with the feta cheese and dill. Garnish with the parsley and serve immediately.

Nutrition Info:

- Info Per Serving: Calories: 565;Fat: 17.8g;Protein: 63.3g;Carbs: 43.9g.

Instant Pot Poached Salmon

Servings:4
Cooking Time: 3 Minutes

Ingredients:

- 1 lemon, sliced ¼ inch thick
- 4 skinless salmon fillets, 1½ inches thick
- ½ teaspoon salt
- ¼ teaspoon pepper
- ½ cup water

Directions:

1. Layer the lemon slices in the bottom of the Instant Pot.
2. Season the salmon with salt and pepper, then arrange the salmon (skin- side down) on top of the lemon slices. Pour in the water.
3. Secure the lid. Select the Manual mode and set the cooking time for 3 minutes at High Pressure.
4. Once cooking is complete, do a quick pressure release. Carefully open the lid.
5. Serve warm.

Nutrition Info:

- Info Per Serving: Calories: 350;Fat: 23.0g;Protein: 35.0g;Carbs: 0g.

Better-for-you Cod & Potatoes

Servings:4
Cooking Time:35 Minutes

Ingredients:

- 1 tbsp olive oil
- 2 cod fillets
- 1 tbsp basil, chopped
- Salt and black pepper to taste
- 2 potatoes, peeled and sliced
- 2 tsp turmeric powder
- 1 garlic clove, minced

Directions:

1. Preheat the oven to 360F. Spread the potatoes on a greased baking dish and season with salt and pepper. Bake for 10 minutes. Arrange the cod fillets on top of the potatoes, sprinkle with salt and pepper, and drizzle with some olive oil. Bake for 10-12 more minutes until the fish flakes easily.
2. Warm the remaining olive oil in a skillet over medium heat and sauté garlic for 1 minute. Stir in basil, salt, pepper, turmeric powder, and 3-4 tbsp of water; cook for another 2-3 minutes. Pour the sauce over the cod fillets and serve warm.

Nutrition Info:

- Info Per Serving: Calories: 300;Fat: 15g;Protein: 33g;Carbs: 28g.

Shrimp & Gnocchi With Feta Cheese

Servings:4
Cooking Time:30 Minutes

Ingredients:

- 1 lb shrimp, shells and tails removed
- 1 jar roasted red peppers, chopped
- 2 tbsp olive oil
- 1 cup chopped fresh tomato
- 2 garlic cloves, minced
- ½ tsp dried oregano
- Black pepper to taste
- ¼ tsp crushed red peppers
- 1 lb potato gnocchi
- ½ cup cubed feta cheese
- ⅓ cup fresh basil leaves, torn

Directions:

1. Preheat oven to 425 F. In a baking dish, mix the tomatoes, olive oil, garlic, oregano, black pepper, and crushed red peppers. Roast in the oven for 10 minutes. Stir in the roasted peppers and shrimp. Roast for 10 minutes until the shrimp turn pink. Bring a saucepan of salted water to the boil and cook the gnocchi for 1-2 mins, until floating. Drain. Remove the dish from the oven. Mix in the cooked gnocchi, sprinkle with feta and basil and serve.

Nutrition Info:

- Info Per Serving: Calories: 146;Fat: 5g;Protein: 23g;Carbs: 1g.

Drunken Mussels With Lemon-butter Sauce

Servings:4
Cooking Time:15 Minutes

Ingredients:

- 4 lb mussels, cleaned
- 4 tbsp butter
- ½ cup chopped parsley
- 1 white onion, chopped
- 2 cups dry white wine
- ½ tsp sea salt
- 6 garlic cloves, minced
- Juice of ½ lemon

Directions:

1. Add wine, garlic, salt, onion, and ¼ cup of parsley in a pot over medium heat and let simmer. Put in mussels and simmer covered for 7-8 minutes. Divide mussels between four bowls. Stir butter and lemon juice into the pot and drizzle over the mussels. Top with parsley and serve.

Nutrition Info:

- Info Per Serving: Calories: 487;Fat: 18g;Protein: 37g;Carbs: 26g.

Dill Chutney Salmon

Servings:2
Cooking Time: 3 Minutes

Ingredients:

- Chutney:
- ¼ cup fresh dill
- ¼ cup extra virgin olive oil
- Juice from ½ lemon
- Sea salt, to taste
- Fish:
- 2 cups water
- 2 salmon fillets
- Juice from ½ lemon
- ¼ teaspoon paprika
- Salt and freshly ground pepper to taste

Directions:

1. Pulse all the chutney ingredients in a food processor until creamy. Set aside.
2. Add the water and steamer basket to the Instant Pot. Place salmon fillets, skin-side down, on the steamer basket. Drizzle the lemon juice over salmon and sprinkle with the paprika.
3. Secure the lid. Select the Manual mode and set the cooking time for 3 minutes at High Pressure.
4. Once cooking is complete, do a quick pressure release. Carefully open the lid.
5. Season the fillets with pepper and salt to taste. Serve topped with the dill chutney.

Nutrition Info:

- Info Per Serving: Calories: 636;Fat: 41.1g;Protein: 65.3g;Carbs: 1.9g.

Parsley Halibut With Roasted Peppers

Servings:4
Cooking Time:45 Minutes

Ingredients:

- 3 tbsp olive oil
- 1 tsp butter
- 2 red peppers, cut into wedges
- 4 halibut fillets
- 2 shallots, cut into rings
- 2 garlic cloves, minced
- ¾ cup breadcrumbs
- 2 tbsp chopped fresh parsley
- Salt and black pepper to taste

Directions:

1. Preheat oven to 450 F. Combine red peppers, garlic, shallots, 1 tbsp of olive oil, salt, and pepper in a bowl. Spread on a baking sheet and bake for 40 minutes. Warm the remaining olive oil in a pan over medium heat and brown the breadcrumbs for 4-5 minutes, stirring constantly. Set aside.
2. Clean the pan and add in the butter to melt. Sprinkle the fish with salt and pepper. Add to the butter and cook for 8-10 minutes on both sides. Divide the pepper mixture between 4 plates and top with halibut fillets. Spread the crunchy breadcrumbs all over and top with parsley. Serve and enjoy!

Nutrition Info:

- Info Per Serving: Calories: 511;Fat: 19.4g;Protein: 64g;Carbs: 18g.

Lemon Shrimp With Black Olives

Servings:4
Cooking Time:25 Minutes

Ingredients:

- 1 lb shrimp, peeled and deveined
- 3 tbsp olive oil
- 1 lemon, juiced
- 1 tbsp flour
- 1 cup fish stock
- Salt and black pepper to taste
- 1 cup black olives, halved
- 1 tbsp rosemary, chopped

Directions:

1. Warm the olive oil in a skillet over medium heat and sear shrimp for 4 minutes on both sides; set aside. In the same skillet over low heat, stir in the flour for 2-3 minutes.
2. Gradually pour in the fish stock and lemon juice while stirring and simmer for 3-4 minutes until the sauce thickens. Adjust the seasoning with salt and pepper and mix in shrimp, olives, and rosemary. Serve immediately.

Nutrition Info:

- Info Per Serving: Calories: 240;Fat: 16g;Protein: 9g;Carbs: 16g.

Asian-inspired Tuna Lettuce Wraps

Servings:2
Cooking Time: 0 Minutes

Ingredients:

- ⅓ cup almond butter
- 1 tablespoon freshly squeezed lemon juice
- 1 teaspoon low-sodium soy sauce
- 1 teaspoon curry powder
- ½ teaspoon sriracha, or to taste
- ½ cup canned water chestnuts, drained and chopped
- 2 package tuna packed in water, drained
- 2 large butter lettuce leaves

Directions:

1. Stir together the almond butter, lemon juice, soy sauce, curry powder, sriracha in a medium bowl until well mixed. Add the water chestnuts and tuna and stir until well incorporated.
2. Place 2 butter lettuce leaves on a flat work surface, spoon half of the tuna mixture onto each leaf and roll up into a wrap. Serve immediately.

Nutrition Info:

- Info Per Serving: Calories: 270;Fat: 13.9g;Protein: 19.1g;Carbs: 18.5g.

Scallion Clams With Snow Peas

Servings:4
Cooking Time:30 Minutes

Ingredients:

- 2 tbsp olive oil
- 1 tbsp basil, chopped
- 2 lb clams
- 1 onion, chopped
- 4 garlic cloves, minced
- Salt and black pepper to taste
- ½ cup vegetable stock

- 1 cup snow peas, sliced
- ½ tbsp balsamic vinegar
- 1 cup scallions, sliced

Directions:

1. Warm olive oil in a skillet over medium heat. Sauté onion and garlic for 2 to 3 minutes until tender and fragrant, stirring often. Add in the clams, salt, pepper, vegetable stock, snow peas, balsamic vinegar, and basil and bring to a boil. Lower the heat and simmer for 10 minutes. Remove from the heat. Discard any unopened clams. Scatter with scallions.

Nutrition Info:

- Info Per Serving: Calories: 310;Fat: 13g;Protein: 22g;Carbs: 27g.

Cioppino (seafood Tomato Stew)

Servings:2
Cooking Time: 20 Minutes

Ingredients:

- 2 tablespoons olive oil
- ½ small onion, diced
- ½ green pepper, diced
- 2 teaspoons dried basil
- 2 teaspoons dried oregano
- ½ cup dry white wine
- 1 can diced tomatoes with basil
- 1 can no-salt-added tomato sauce
- 1 can minced clams with their juice
- 8 ounces peeled, deveined raw shrimp
- 4 ounces any white fish (a thick piece works best)
- 3 tablespoons fresh parsley
- Salt and freshly ground black pepper, to taste

Directions:

1. In a Dutch oven, heat the olive oil over medium heat.
2. Sauté the onion and green pepper for 5 minutes, or until tender.
3. Stir in the basil, oregano, wine, diced tomatoes, and tomato sauce and bring to a boil.
4. Once boiling, reduce the heat to low and bring to a simmer for 5 minutes.
5. Add the clams, shrimp, and fish and cook for about 10 minutes, or until the shrimp are pink and cooked through.
6. Scatter with the parsley and add the salt and black pepper to taste.
7. Remove from the heat and serve warm.

Nutrition Info:

- Info Per Serving: Calories: 221;Fat: 7.7g;Protein: 23.1g;Carbs: 10.9g.

Honey-mustard Roasted Salmon

Servings:4
Cooking Time: 15 To 20 Minutes

Ingredients:

- 2 tablespoons whole-grain mustard
- 2 garlic cloves, minced
- 1 tablespoon honey
- ¼ teaspoon salt
- ¼ teaspoon freshly ground black pepper
- 1 pound salmon fillet
- Nonstick cooking spray

Directions:

1. Preheat the oven to 425°F. Coat a baking sheet with nonstick cooking spray.
2. Stir together the mustard, garlic, honey, salt, and pepper in a small bowl.
3. Arrange the salmon fillet, skin-side down, on the coated baking sheet. Spread the mustard mixture evenly over the salmon fillet.
4. Roast in the preheated oven for 15 to 20 minutes, or until it flakes apart easily and reaches an internal temperature of 145°F.
5. Serve hot.

Nutrition Info:

- Info Per Serving: Calories: 185;Fat: 7.0g;Protein: 23.2g;Carbs: 5.8g.

Herby Tuna Gratin

Servings:4
Cooking Time:20 Minutes

Ingredients:

- 10 oz canned tuna, flaked
- 4 eggs, whisked
- ½ cup mozzarella, shredded
- 1 tbsp chives, chopped
- 1 tbsp parsley, chopped
- Salt and black pepper to taste

Directions:

1. Preheat the oven to 360 F. Mix tuna, eggs, chives, parsley, salt, and pepper in a bowl. Transfer to a greased baking dish and bake for 15 minutes. Scatter cheese on top and let sit for 5 minutes. Cut before

serving.

Nutrition Info:

• Info Per Serving: Calories: 300;Fat: 15g;Protein: 7g;Carbs: 13g.

Avocado Shrimp Ceviche

Servings:4
Cooking Time: 0 Minutes

Ingredients:

• 1 pound fresh shrimp, peeled, deveined, and cut in half lengthwise
• 1 small red or yellow bell pepper, cut into ½-inch chunks
• ½ small red onion, cut into thin slivers
• ½ English cucumber, peeled and cut into ½-inch chunks
• ¼ cup chopped fresh cilantro
• ½ cup extra-virgin olive oil
• ⅓ cup freshly squeezed lime juice
• 2 tablespoons freshly squeezed clementine juice
• 2 tablespoons freshly squeezed lemon juice
• 1 teaspoon salt
• ½ teaspoon freshly ground black pepper
• 2 ripe avocados, peeled, pitted, and cut into ½-inch chunks

Directions:

1. Place the shrimp, bell pepper, red onion, cucumber, and cilantro in a large bowl and toss to combine.
2. In a separate bowl, stir together the olive oil, lime, clementine, and lemon juice, salt, and black pepper until smooth. Pour the mixture into the bowl of shrimp and vegetable mixture and toss until they are completely coated.
3. Cover the bowl with plastic wrap and transfer to the refrigerator to marinate for at least 2 hours, or up to 8 hours.
4. When ready, stir in the avocado chunks and toss to incorporate. Serve immediately.

Nutrition Info:

• Info Per Serving: Calories: 496;Fat: 39.5g;Protein: 25.3g;Carbs: 13.8g.

Spicy Haddock Stew

Servings:6
Cooking Time: 35 Minutes

Ingredients:

• ¼ cup coconut oil
• 1 tablespoon minced garlic
• 1 onion, chopped
• 2 celery stalks, chopped
• ½ fennel bulb, thinly sliced
• 1 carrot, diced
• 1 sweet potato, diced
• 1 can low-sodium diced tomatoes
• 1 cup coconut milk
• 1 cup low-sodium chicken broth
• ¼ teaspoon red pepper flakes
• 12 ounces haddock, cut into 1-inch chunks
• 2 tablespoons chopped fresh cilantro, for garnish

Directions:

1. In a large saucepan, heat the coconut oil over medium-high heat.
2. Add the garlic, onion, and celery and sauté for about 4 minutes, stirring occasionally, or until they are tender.
3. Stir in the fennel bulb, carrot, and sweet potato and sauté for 4 minutes more.
4. Add the diced tomatoes, coconut milk, chicken broth, and red pepper flakes and stir to incorporate, then bring the mixture to a boil.
5. Once it starts to boil, reduce the heat to low, and bring to a simmer for about 15 minutes, or until the vegetables are fork-tender.
6. Add the haddock chunks and continue simmering for about 10 minutes, or until the fish is cooked through.
7. Sprinkle the cilantro on top for garnish before serving.

Nutrition Info:

• Info Per Serving: Calories: 276;Fat: 20.9g;Protein: 14.2g;Carbs: 6.8g.

Dill Smoked Salmon & Eggplant Rolls

Servings:4
Cooking Time:20 Minutes

Ingredients:

- 2 eggplants, lengthwise cut into thin slices
- 2 tbsp olive oil
- 1 cup ricotta cheese, soft
- 4 oz smoked salmon, chopped
- 2 tsp lemon zest, grated
- 1 small red onion, sliced
- Salt and pepper to the taste

Directions:

1. Mix salmon, cheese, lemon zest, onion, salt, and pepper in a bowl. Grease the eggplant with olive oil and grill them on a preheated grill pan for 3-4 minutes per side. Set aside to cool. Spread the cooled eggplant slices with the salmon mixture. Roll out and secure with toothpicks and serve.

Nutrition Info:

- Info Per Serving: Calories: 310;Fat: 25g;Protein: 12g;Carbs: 16g.

Calamari In Garlic-cilantro Sauce

Servings:4
Cooking Time:25 Minutes

Ingredients:

- 2 tbsp olive oil
- 2 lb calamari, sliced into rings
- 4 garlic cloves, minced
- 1 lime, juiced
- 2 tbsp balsamic vinegar
- 3 tbsp cilantro, chopped

Directions:

1. Warm the olive oil in a skillet over medium heat and sauté garlic, lime juice, balsamic vinegar, and cilantro for 5 minutes. Stir in calamari rings and cook for 10 minutes.

Nutrition Info:

- Info Per Serving: Calories: 290;Fat: 19g;Protein: 19g;Carbs: 10g.

Mom's Cod With Mozzarella & Tomatoes

Servings:4
Cooking Time:35 Minutes

Ingredients:

- 2 tbsp olive oil
- 4 cod fillets, boneless
- Salt and black pepper to taste
- 12 cherry tomatoes, halved
- 1 red chili pepper, chopped
- 1 tbsp cilantro, chopped
- 2 tbsp balsamic vinegar
- 1 oz fresh mozzarella, torn

Directions:

1. Preheat the oven to 380 F. Drizzle the cod fillets with some olive oil and season with salt and pepper. Place them on a roasting tray, top with mozzarella cheese, and bake for 15 minutes until golden and crispy. Warm the remaining oil in a skillet over medium heat and cook the cherry tomatoes for 5 minutes. Stir in red chili pepper, cilantro, and balsamic vinegar for 1-2 minutes. Serve the fish with sautéed veggies.

Nutrition Info:

- Info Per Serving: Calories: 270;Fat: 11g;Protein: 21g;Carbs: 25g.

Walnut-crusted Salmon

Servings:4
Cooking Time:25 Minutes

Ingredients:

- 2 tbsp olive oil
- 4 salmon fillets, boneless
- 2 tbsp mustard
- 5 tsp honey
- 1 cup walnuts, chopped
- 1 tbsp lemon juice
- 2 tsp parsley, chopped
- Salt and pepper to the taste

Directions:

1. Preheat the oven to 380F. Line a baking tray with parchment paper. In a bowl, whisk the olive oil, mustard, and honey. In a separate bowl, combine walnuts and parsley. Sprinkle salmon with salt and pepper and place them on the tray. Rub each fillet with mustard mixture and scatter with walnut mixture; bake for 15

minutes. Drizzle with lemon juice.

Nutrition Info:

- Info Per Serving: Calories: 300;Fat: 16g;Protein: 17g;Carbs: 22g.

Spicy Cod Fillets

Servings:4
Cooking Time:35 Minutes

Ingredients:

- 2 tbsp olive oil
- 1 tsp lime juice
- Salt and black pepper to taste
- 1 tsp sweet paprika
- 1 tsp chili powder
- 1 onion, chopped
- 2 garlic cloves, minced
- 4 cod fillets, boneless
- 1 tsp ground coriander
- ½ cup fish stock
- ½ lb cherry tomatoes, cubed

Directions:

1. Warm olive oil in a skillet over medium heat. Season the cod with salt, pepper, and chili powder and cook in the skillet for 8 minutes on all sides; set aside. In the same skillet, cook onion and garlic for 3 minutes. Stir in lime juice, paprika, coriander, fish stock, and cherry tomatoes and bring to a boil. Simmer for 10 minutes. Serve topped with cod fillets.

Nutrition Info:

- Info Per Serving: Calories: 240;Fat: 17g;Protein: 17g;Carbs: 26g.

Dill Baked Sea Bass

Servings:6
Cooking Time: 10 To 15 Minutes

Ingredients:

- ¼ cup olive oil
- 2 pounds sea bass
- Sea salt and freshly ground pepper, to taste
- 1 garlic clove, minced
- ¼ cup dry white wine
- 3 teaspoons fresh dill
- 2 teaspoons fresh thyme

Directions:

1. Preheat the oven to 425°F.
2. Brush the bottom of a roasting pan with the olive oil. Place the fish in the pan and brush the fish with oil.
3. Season the fish with sea salt and freshly ground pepper. Combine the remaining ingredients and pour over the fish.
4. Bake in the preheated oven for 10 to 15 minutes, depending on the size of the fish.
5. Serve hot.

Nutrition Info:

- Info Per Serving: Calories: 224;Fat: 12.1g;Protein: 28.1g;Carbs: 0.9g.

Vegetable Mains And Meatless Recipes

Roasted Vegetables

Servings:2
Cooking Time: 35 Minutes

Ingredients:

- 6 teaspoons extra-virgin olive oil, divided
- 12 to 15 Brussels sprouts, halved
- 1 medium sweet potato, peeled and cut into 2-inch cubes
- 2 cups fresh cauliflower florets
- 1 medium zucchini, cut into 1-inch rounds
- 1 red bell pepper, cut into 1-inch slices
- Salt, to taste

Directions:

1. Preheat the oven to 425°F.
2. Add 2 teaspoons of olive oil, Brussels sprouts, sweet potato, and salt to a large bowl and toss until they are completely coated.
3. Transfer them to a large roasting pan and roast for 10 minutes, or until the Brussels sprouts are lightly browned.
4. Meantime, combine the cauliflower florets with 2 teaspoons of olive oil and salt in a separate bowl.
5. Remove from the oven. Add the cauliflower florets to the roasting pan and roast for 10 minutes more.
6. Meanwhile, toss the zucchini and bell pepper with the remaining olive oil in a medium bowl until well coated. Season with salt.
7. Remove the roasting pan from the oven and stir in the zucchini and bell pepper. Continue roasting for 15 minutes, or until the vegetables are fork-tender.
8. Divide the roasted vegetables between two plates and serve warm.

Nutrition Info:

- Info Per Serving: Calories: 333;Fat: 16.8g;Protein: 12.2g;Carbs: 37.6g.

Veggie Rice Bowls With Pesto Sauce

Servings:2
Cooking Time: 1 Minute

Ingredients:

- 2 cups water
- 1 cup arborio rice, rinsed
- Salt and ground black pepper, to taste
- 2 eggs
- 1 cup broccoli florets
- ½ pound Brussels sprouts
- 1 carrot, peeled and chopped
- 1 small beet, peeled and cubed
- ¼ cup pesto sauce
- Lemon wedges, for serving

Directions:

1. Combine the water, rice, salt, and pepper in the Instant Pot. Insert a trivet over rice and place a steamer basket on top. Add the eggs, broccoli, Brussels sprouts, carrots, beet cubes, salt, and pepper to the steamer basket.
2. Lock the lid. Select the Manual mode and set the cooking time for 1 minute at High Pressure.
3. When the timer beeps, perform a natural pressure release for 10 minutes, then release any remaining pressure. Carefully open the lid.
4. Remove the steamer basket and trivet from the pot and transfer the eggs to a bowl of ice water. Peel and halve the eggs. Use a fork to fluff the rice.
5. Divide the rice, broccoli, Brussels sprouts, carrot, beet cubes, and eggs into two bowls. Top with a dollop of pesto sauce and serve with the lemon wedges.

Nutrition Info:

- Info Per Serving: Calories: 590;Fat: 34.1g;Protein: 21.9g;Carbs: 50.0g.

Baked Potato With Veggie Mix

Servings:4
Cooking Time:45 Minutes

Ingredients:

- 4 tbsp olive oil
- 1 lb potatoes, peeled and diced
- 2 red bell peppers, halved
- 1 lb mushrooms, sliced
- 2 tomatoes, diced
- 8 garlic cloves, peeled
- 1 eggplant, sliced
- 1 yellow onion, quartered
- ½ tsp dried oregano
- ¼ tsp caraway seeds
- Salt to taste

Directions:

1. Preheat the oven to 390 F. In a bowl, combine the bell peppers, mushrooms, tomatoes, eggplant, onion, garlic, salt, olive oil, oregano, and caraway seeds. Set aside. Arrange the potatoes on a baking dish and bake for 15 minutes. Top with the veggies mixture and bake for 15-20 minutes until tender.

Nutrition Info:

- Info Per Serving: Calories: 302;Fat: 15g;Protein: 8.5g;Carbs: 39g.

Roasted Vegetable Medley

Servings:2
Cooking Time:65 Minutes

Ingredients:

- 1 head garlic, cloves split apart, unpeeled
- 3 tbsp olive oil
- 2 carrots, cut into strips
- ¼ lb asparagus, chopped
- ½ lb Brussels sprouts, halved
- 2 cups broccoli florets
- 1 cup cherry tomatoes
- ½ fresh lemon, sliced
- Salt and black pepper to taste

Directions:

1. Preheat oven to 375 F. Drizzle the garlic cloves with some olive oil and lightly wrap them in a small piece of foil. Place the packet in the oven and roast for 30 minutes. Place all the vegetables and the lemon slices into a large mixing bowl. Drizzle with the remaining olive oil and season with salt and pepper. Increase the oven to 400 F. Pour the vegetables on a sheet pan in a single layer, leaving the packet of garlic cloves on the pan. Roast for 20 minutes, shaking occasionally until tender. Remove the pan from the oven. Let the garlic cloves sit until cool enough to handle, then remove the skins. Top the vegetables with roasted garlic and serve.

Nutrition Info:

- Info Per Serving: Calories: 256;Fat: 15g;Protein: 7g;Carbs: 31g.

Tasty Lentil Burgers

Servings:4
Cooking Time:25 Minutes

Ingredients:

- 1 cup cremini mushrooms, finely chopped
- 1 cup cooked green lentils
- ½ cup Greek yogurt
- ½ lemon, zested and juiced
- ½ tsp garlic powder
- ½ tsp dried oregano
- 1 tbsp fresh cilantro, chopped
- Salt to taste
- 3 tbsp extra-virgin olive oil
- ¼ tsp tbsp white miso
- ¼ tsp smoked paprika
- ¼ cup flour

Directions:

1. Pour ½ cup of lentils in your blender and puree partially until somewhat smooth, but with many whole lentils still remaining. In a small bowl, mix the yogurt, lemon zest and juice, garlic powder, oregano, cilantro, and salt. Season and set aside. In a medium bowl, mix the mushrooms, 2 tablespoons of olive oil, miso, and paprika. Stir in all the lentils. Add in flour and stir until the mixture everything is well incorporated. Shape the mixture into patties about ¾-inch thick. Warm the remaining olive oil in a skillet over medium heat. Fry the patties until browned and crisp, about 3 minutes. Turn and fry on the second side. Serve with the reserved yogurt mixture.

Nutrition Info:

- Info Per Serving: Calories: 215;Fat: 13g;Protein: 10g;Carbs: 19g.

Paprika Cauliflower Steaks With Walnut Sauce

Servings:2
Cooking Time: 30 Minutes

Ingredients:

- Walnut Sauce:
- ½ cup raw walnut halves
- 2 tablespoons virgin olive oil, divided
- 1 clove garlic, chopped
- 1 small yellow onion, chopped
- ½ cup unsweetened almond milk
- 2 tablespoons fresh lemon juice
- Salt and pepper, to taste
- Paprika Cauliflower:
- 1 medium head cauliflower
- 1 teaspoon sweet paprika
- 1 teaspoon minced fresh thyme leaves

Directions:

1. Preheat the oven to 350ºF.
2. Make the walnut sauce: Toast the walnuts in a large, ovenproof skillet over medium heat until fragrant and slightly darkened, about 5 minutes. Transfer the walnuts to a blender.
3. Heat 1 tablespoon of olive oil in the skillet. Add the garlic and onion and sauté for about 2 minutes, or until slightly softened. Transfer the garlic and onion into the blender, along with the almond milk, lemon juice, salt, and pepper. Blend the ingredients until smooth and creamy. Keep the sauce warm while you prepare the cauliflower.
4. Make the paprika cauliflower: Cut two 1-inch-thick "steaks" from the center of the cauliflower. Lightly moisten the steaks with water and season both sides with paprika, thyme, salt, and pepper.
5. Heat the remaining 1 tablespoon of olive oil in the skillet over medium-high heat. Add the cauliflower steaks and sear for about 3 minutes until evenly browned. Flip the cauliflower steaks and transfer the skillet to the oven.
6. Roast in the preheated oven for about 20 minutes until crisp-tender.
7. Serve the cauliflower steaks warm with the walnut sauce on the side.

Nutrition Info:

- Info Per Serving: Calories: 367;Fat: 27.9g;Protein: 7.0g;Carbs: 22.7g.

Sweet Potato Chickpea Buddha Bowl

Servings:2
Cooking Time: 10 To 15 Minutes

Ingredients:

- Sauce:
- 1 tablespoon tahini
- 2 tablespoons plain Greek yogurt
- 2 tablespoons hemp seeds
- 1 garlic clove, minced
- Pinch salt
- Freshly ground black pepper, to taste
- Bowl:
- 1 small sweet potato, peeled and finely diced
- 1 teaspoon extra-virgin olive oil
- 1 cup from 1 can low-sodium chickpeas, drained and rinsed
- 2 cups baby kale

Directions:

1. Make the Sauce
2. Whisk together the tahini and yogurt in a small bowl.
3. Stir in the hemp seeds and minced garlic. Season with salt pepper. Add 2 to 3 tablespoons water to create a creamy yet pourable consistency and set aside.
4. Make the Bowl
5. Preheat the oven to 425ºF. Line a baking sheet with parchment paper.
6. Place the sweet potato on the prepared baking sheet and drizzle with the olive oil. Toss well
7. Roast in the preheated oven for 10 to 15 minutes, stirring once during cooking, or until fork-tender and browned.
8. In each of 2 bowls, place ½ cup of chickpeas, 1 cup of baby kale, and half of the cooked sweet potato. Serve drizzled with half of the prepared sauce.

Nutrition Info:

- Info Per Serving: Calories: 323;Fat: 14.1g;Protein: 17.0g;Carbs: 36.0g.

Fish & Chickpea Stew

Servings:4
Cooking Time:30 Minutes

Ingredients:

- 3 tbsp olive oil
- 1 lb tilapia fish, cubed
- 1 lb canned chickpeas
- 1 cup canned tomatoes
- 1 parsnip, chopped
- 1 bell pepper, chopped
- ½ cup shallots, chopped
- 1 tsp garlic puree
- ½ tsp dried basil
- 1 bay leaf
- ¼ cup dry white wine
- 1 cup fish stock
- 2 cups vegetable broth
- Salt and black pepper to taste

Directions:

1. Warm the oil in a pot over medium heat. Add in parsnip, bell pepper, garlic, and shallots and cook for 3-5 minutes. Add in basil and bay leaf. Cook for another 30-40 seconds. Pour in white wine to scrape off any bits from the bottom.
2. Stir in fish stock, vegetable broth, and tomatoes. Bring to a boil, lower the heat, and simmer for 10 minutes. Mix in fish, chickpeas, salt, and black pepper. Simmer covered for 10 minutes more. Adjust the taste and discard the bay leaf.

Nutrition Info:

- Info Per Serving: Calories: 469;Fat: 13g;Protein: 34g;Carbs: 55g.

Italian Hot Green Beans

Servings:4
Cooking Time:25 Minutes

Ingredients:

- 2 tbsp olive oil
- 1 red bell pepper, diced
- 1 ½ lb green beans
- 4 garlic cloves, minced
- ½ tsp mustard seeds
- ½ tsp fennel seeds
- 1 tsp dried dill weed
- 2 tomatoes, chopped
- 1 cup cream of celery soup
- 1 tsp Italian herb mix
- 1 tsp chili powder
- Salt and black pepper to taste

Directions:

1. Warm the olive oil in a saucepan over medium heat. Add and fry the bell pepper and green beans for about 5 minutes, stirring periodically to promote even cooking. Add in the garlic, mustard seeds, fennel seeds, and dill and continue sautéing for an additional 1 minute or until fragrant. Add in the pureed tomatoes, cream of celery soup, Italian herb mix, chili powder, salt, and black pepper. Continue to simmer, covered, for 10-12 minutes until the green beans are tender.

Nutrition Info:

- Info Per Serving: Calories: 160;Fat: 9g;Protein: 5g;Carbs: 19g.

Roasted Vegetables And Chickpeas

Servings:2
Cooking Time: 30 Minutes

Ingredients:

- 4 cups cauliflower florets (about ½ small head)
- 2 medium carrots, peeled, halved, and then sliced into quarters lengthwise
- 2 tablespoons olive oil, divided
- ½ teaspoon garlic powder, divided
- ½ teaspoon salt, divided
- 2 teaspoons za'atar spice mix, divided
- 1 can chickpeas, drained, rinsed, and patted dry
- ¾ cup plain Greek yogurt
- 1 teaspoon harissa spice paste

Directions:

1. Preheat the oven to 400°F. Line a sheet pan with foil or parchment paper.
2. Place the cauliflower and carrots in a large bowl. Drizzle with 1 tablespoon olive oil and sprinkle with ¼ teaspoon of garlic powder, ¼ teaspoon of salt, and 1 teaspoon of za'atar. Toss well to combine.
3. Spread the vegetables onto one half of the sheet pan in a single layer.
4. Place the chickpeas in the same bowl and season with the remaining 1 tablespoon of oil, ¼ teaspoon of garlic powder, and ¼ teaspoon of salt, and the remaining za'atar. Toss well to combine.
5. Spread the chickpeas onto the other half of the sheet pan.
6. Roast for 30 minutes, or until the vegetables are

tender and the chickpeas start to turn golden. Flip the vegetables halfway through the cooking time, and give the chickpeas a stir so they cook evenly.

7. The chickpeas may need an extra few minutes if you like them crispy. If so, remove the vegetables and leave the chickpeas in until they're cooked to desired crispiness.

8. Meanwhile, combine the yogurt and harissa in a small bowl. Taste and add additional harissa as desired, then serve.

Nutrition Info:

- Info Per Serving: Calories: 468;Fat: 23.0g;Protein: 18.1g;Carbs: 54.1g.

Spicy Potato Wedges

Servings:4
Cooking Time:30 Minutes

Ingredients:

- 1 ½ lb potatoes, peeled and cut into wedges
- 3 tbsp olive oil
- 1 tbsp minced fresh rosemary
- 2 tsp chili powder
- 3 garlic cloves, minced
- Salt and black pepper to taste

Directions:

1. Preheat the oven to 370 F. Toss the wedges with olive oil, garlic, salt, and pepper. Spread out in a roasting sheet. Roast for 15-20 minutes until browned and crisp at the edges. Remove and sprinkle with chili powder and rosemary.

Nutrition Info:

- Info Per Serving: Calories: 152;Fat: 7g;Protein: 2.5g;Carbs: 21g.

Baked Vegetable Stew

Servings:6
Cooking Time:70 Minutes

Ingredients:

- 1 can diced tomatoes, drained with juice reserved
- 3 tbsp olive oil
- 1 onion, chopped
- 2 tbsp fresh oregano, minced
- 1 tsp paprika
- 4 garlic cloves, minced
- 1 ½ lb green beans, sliced
- 1 lb Yukon Gold potatoes, peeled and chopped
- 1 tbsp tomato paste
- Salt and black pepper to taste
- 3 tbsp fresh basil, chopped

Directions:

1. Preheat oven to 360 F. Warm the olive oil in a skillet over medium heat. Sauté onion and garlic for 3 minutes until softened. Stir in oregano and paprika for 30 seconds. Transfer to a baking dish and add in green beans, potatoes, tomatoes, tomato paste, salt, pepper, and 1 ½ cups of water; stir well. Bake for 40-50 minutes. Sprinkle with basil. Serve.

Nutrition Info:

- Info Per Serving: Calories: 121;Fat: 0.8g;Protein: 4.2g;Carbs: 26g.

Creamy Polenta With Mushrooms

Servings:2
Cooking Time: 30 Minutes

Ingredients:

- ½ ounce dried porcini mushrooms (optional but recommended)
- 2 tablespoons olive oil
- 1 pound baby bella (cremini) mushrooms, quartered
- 1 large shallot, minced
- 1 garlic clove, minced
- 1 tablespoon flour
- 2 teaspoons tomato paste
- ½ cup red wine
- 1 cup mushroom stock (or reserved liquid from soaking the porcini mushrooms, if using)
- ½ teaspoon dried thyme
- 1 fresh rosemary sprig
- 1½ cups water
- ½ teaspoon salt
- ⅓ cup instant polenta
- 2 tablespoons grated Parmesan cheese

Directions:

1. If using the dried porcini mushrooms, soak them in 1 cup of hot water for about 15 minutes to soften them. When they're softened, scoop them out of the water, reserving the soaking liquid. Mince the porcini mushrooms.

2. Heat the olive oil in a large sauté pan over medium-high heat. Add the mushrooms, shallot, and garlic, and sauté for 10 minutes, or until the vegetables are wilted and starting to caramelize.

3. Add the flour and tomato paste, and cook for anoth-

er 30 seconds. Add the red wine, mushroom stock or porcini soaking liquid, thyme, and rosemary. Bring the mixture to a boil, stirring constantly until it thickens. Reduce the heat and let it simmer for 10 minutes.

4. Meanwhile, bring the water to a boil in a saucepan and add salt.

5. Add the instant polenta and stir quickly while it thickens. Stir in the Parmesan cheese. Taste and add additional salt, if needed. Serve warm.

Nutrition Info:

- Info Per Serving: Calories: 450;Fat: 16.0g;Protein: 14.1g;Carbs: 57.8g.

Grilled Eggplant "steaks" With Sauce

Servings:6
Cooking Time:20 Minutes

Ingredients:

- 2 lb eggplants, sliced lengthways
- 6 tbsp olive oil
- 5 garlic cloves, minced
- 1 tsp dried oregano
- ½ tsp red pepper flakes
- ½ cup Greek yogurt
- 3 tbsp chopped fresh parsley
- 1 tsp grated lemon zest
- 2 tsp lemon juice
- 1 tsp ground cumin
- Salt and black pepper to taste

Directions:

1. In a bowl, whisk half of the olive oil, yogurt, parsley, lemon zest and juice, cumin, and salt; set aside until ready to serve. Preheat your grill to High. Rub the eggplant steaks with the remaining olive oil, oregano, salt, and pepper. Grill them for 4-6 minutes per side until browned and tender; transfer to a serving platter. Drizzle yogurt sauce over eggplant.

Nutrition Info:

- Info Per Serving: Calories: 112;Fat: 7g;Protein: 2.6g;Carbs: 11.3g.

Butternut Noodles With Mushrooms

Servings:4
Cooking Time: 12 Minutes

Ingredients:

- ¼ cup extra-virgin olive oil
- 1 pound cremini mushrooms, sliced
- ½ red onion, finely chopped
- 1 teaspoon dried thyme
- ½ teaspoon sea salt
- 3 garlic cloves, minced
- ½ cup dry white wine
- Pinch of red pepper flakes
- 4 cups butternut noodles
- 4 ounces grated Parmesan cheese

Directions:

1. In a large skillet over medium-high heat, heat the olive oil until shimmering. Add the mushrooms, onion, thyme, and salt to the skillet. Cook for about 6 minutes, stirring occasionally, or until the mushrooms start to brown. Add the garlic and sauté for 30 seconds. Stir in the white wine and red pepper flakes.
2. Fold in the noodles. Cook for about 5 minutes, stirring occasionally, or until the noodles are tender.
3. Serve topped with the grated Parmesan.

Nutrition Info:

- Info Per Serving: Calories: 244;Fat: 14.0g;Protein: 4.0g;Carbs: 22.0g.

Wilted Dandelion Greens With Sweet Onion

Servings:4
Cooking Time: 15 Minutes

Ingredients:

- 1 tablespoon extra-virgin olive oil
- 2 garlic cloves, minced
- 1 Vidalia onion, thinly sliced
- ½ cup low-sodium vegetable broth
- 2 bunches dandelion greens, roughly chopped
- Freshly ground black pepper, to taste

Directions:

1. Heat the olive oil in a large skillet over low heat.
2. Add the garlic and onion and cook for 2 to 3 minutes, stirring occasionally, or until the onion is translucent.
3. Fold in the vegetable broth and dandelion greens and cook for 5 to 7 minutes until wilted, stirring frequently.
4. Sprinkle with the black pepper and serve on a plate while warm.

Nutrition Info:

- Info Per Serving: Calories: 81;Fat: 3.9g;Protein: 3.2g;Carbs: 10.8g.

Creamy Cauliflower Chickpea Curry

Servings:4
Cooking Time: 15 Minutes

Ingredients:

- 3 cups fresh or frozen cauliflower florets
- 2 cups unsweetened almond milk
- 1 can low-sodium chickpeas, drained and rinsed
- 1 can coconut milk
- 1 tablespoon curry powder
- ¼ teaspoon garlic powder
- ¼ teaspoon ground ginger
- ⅛ teaspoon onion powder
- ¼ teaspoon salt

Directions:

1. Add the cauliflower florets, almond milk, chickpeas, coconut milk, curry powder, garlic powder, ginger, and onion powder to a large stockpot and stir to combine.
2. Cover and cook over medium-high heat for 10 minutes, stirring occasionally.
3. Reduce the heat to low and continue cooking uncovered for 5 minutes, or until the cauliflower is tender.
4. Sprinkle with the salt and stir well. Serve warm.

Nutrition Info:

- Info Per Serving: Calories: 409;Fat: 29.6g;Protein: 10.0g;Carbs: 29.8g.

Cauliflower Rice Risotto With Mushrooms

Servings:4
Cooking Time: 10 Minutes

Ingredients:

- 1 teaspoon extra-virgin olive oil
- ½ cup chopped portobello mushrooms
- 4 cups cauliflower rice
- ½ cup half-and-half
- ¼ cup low-sodium vegetable broth
- 1 cup shredded Parmesan cheese

Directions:

1. In a medium skillet, heat the olive oil over medium-low heat until shimmering.
2. Add the mushrooms and stir-fry for 3 minutes.
3. Stir in the cauliflower rice, half-and-half, and vegetable broth. Cover and bring to a boil over high heat for 5 minutes, stirring occasionally.
4. Add the Parmesan cheese and stir to combine. Continue cooking for an additional 3 minutes until the cheese is melted.
5. Divide the mixture into four bowls and serve warm.

Nutrition Info:

- Info Per Serving: Calories: 167;Fat: 10.7g;Protein: 12.1g;Carbs: 8.1g.

Garlic-butter Asparagus With Parmesan

Servings:2
Cooking Time: 8 Minutes

Ingredients:

- 1 cup water
- 1 pound asparagus, trimmed
- 2 cloves garlic, chopped
- 3 tablespoons almond butter
- Salt and ground black pepper, to taste
- 3 tablespoons grated Parmesan cheese

Directions:

1. Pour the water into the Instant Pot and insert a trivet.
2. Put the asparagus on a tin foil add the butter and garlic. Season to taste with salt and pepper.
3. Fold over the foil and seal the asparagus inside so the foil doesn't come open. Arrange the asparagus on the trivet.
4. Secure the lid. Select the Manual mode and set the cooking time for 8 minutes at High Pressure.
5. Once cooking is complete, do a quick pressure release. Carefully open the lid.
6. Unwrap the foil packet and serve sprinkled with the Parmesan cheese.

Nutrition Info:

- Info Per Serving: Calories: 243;Fat: 15.7g;Protein: 12.3g;Carbs: 15.3g.

Baked Tomatoes And Chickpeas

Servings:4
Cooking Time: 40 To 45 Minutes

Ingredients:

- 1 tablespoon extra-virgin olive oil
- ½ medium onion, chopped
- 3 garlic cloves, chopped
- ¼ teaspoon ground cumin
- 2 teaspoons smoked paprika
- 2 cans chickpeas, drained and rinsed
- 4 cups halved cherry tomatoes
- ½ cup plain Greek yogurt, for serving
- 1 cup crumbled feta cheese, for serving

Directions:

1. Preheat the oven to 425°F.
2. Heat the olive oil in an ovenproof skillet over medium heat.
3. Add the onion and garlic and sauté for about 5 minutes, stirring occasionally, or until tender and fragrant.
4. Add the paprika and cumin and cook for 2 minutes. Stir in the chickpeas and tomatoes and allow to simmer for 5 to 10 minutes.
5. Transfer the skillet to the preheated oven and roast for 25 to 30 minutes, or until the mixture bubbles and thickens.
6. Remove from the oven and serve topped with yogurt and crumbled feta cheese.

Nutrition Info:

- Info Per Serving: Calories: 411;Fat: 14.9g;Protein: 20.2g;Carbs: 50.7g.

Hot Turnip Chickpeas

Servings:4
Cooking Time:50 Minutes

Ingredients:

- 2 tbsp olive oil
- 2 onions, chopped
- 2 red bell peppers, chopped
- Salt and black pepper to taste
- ¼ cup tomato paste
- 1 jalapeño pepper, minced
- 5 garlic cloves, minced
- ¾ tsp ground cumin
- ¼ tsp cayenne pepper
- 2 cans chickpeas
- 12 oz potatoes, chopped
- ¼ cup chopped fresh parsley
- 1 lemon, juiced

Directions:

1. Warm the olive oil in a saucepan oven over medium heat. Sauté the onions, bell peppers, salt, and pepper for 6 minutes until softened and lightly browned. Stir in tomato paste, jalapeño pepper, garlic, cumin, and cayenne pepper and cook for about 30 seconds until fragrant. Stir in chickpeas and their liquid, potatoes, and 1 cup of water. Bring to simmer and cook for 25-35 minutes until potatoes are tender and the sauce has thickened. Stir in parsley and lemon juice.

Nutrition Info:

- Info Per Serving: Calories: 124;Fat: 5.3g;Protein: 3.7g;Carbs: 17g.

Zucchini Ribbons With Ricotta

Servings:4
Cooking Time:10 Minutes

Ingredients:

- 3 tbsp olive oil
- 1 garlic clove, minced
- 1 tsp lemon zest
- 1 tbsp lemon juice
- 4 zucchinis, cut into ribbons
- Salt and black pepper to taste
- 2 tbsp chopped fresh parsley
- ½ ricotta cheese, crumbled

Directions:

1. Whisk 2 tablespoons oil, garlic, salt, pepper, and lemon zest, and lemon juice in a bowl. Warm the remaining olive oil in a skillet over medium heat. Season the zucchini ribbons with salt and pepper and add them to the skillet; cook for 3-4 minutes per side. Transfer to a serving bowl and drizzle with the dressing, sprinkle with parsley and cheese and serve.

Nutrition Info:

- Info Per Serving: Calories: 134;Fat: 2g;Protein: 2g;-Carbs: 4g.

Vegetable And Tofu Scramble

Servings:2
Cooking Time: 10 Minutes

Ingredients:

- 2 tablespoons extra-virgin olive oil
- ½ red onion, finely chopped
- 1 cup chopped kale
- 8 ounces mushrooms, sliced
- 8 ounces tofu, cut into pieces
- 2 garlic cloves, minced
- Pinch red pepper flakes
- ½ teaspoon sea salt
- ⅛ teaspoon freshly ground black pepper

Directions:

1. Heat the olive oil in a medium nonstick skillet over medium-high heat until shimmering.
2. Add the onion, kale, and mushrooms to the skillet and cook for about 5 minutes, stirring occasionally, or until the vegetables start to brown.
3. Add the tofu and stir-fry for 3 to 4 minutes until softened.
4. Stir in the garlic, red pepper flakes, salt, and black pepper and cook for 30 seconds.
5. Let the mixture cool for 5 minutes before serving.

Nutrition Info:

- Info Per Serving: Calories: 233;Fat: 15.9g;Protein: 13.4g;Carbs: 11.9g.

Baked Veggie Medley

Servings:4
Cooking Time:70 Minutes

Ingredients:

- 2 tbsp olive oil
- ½ lb green beans, trimmed
- 1 tomato, chopped
- 1 potato, sliced
- ½ tbsp tomato paste
- 2 tbsp chopped fresh parsley
- 1 tsp sweet paprika
- 1 onion, sliced
- 1 cup mushrooms, sliced
- 1 celery stalk, chopped
- 1 red bell pepper, sliced
- 1 eggplant, sliced
- ½ cup vegetable broth
- Salt and black pepper to taste

Directions:

1. Preheat oven to 375 F. Warm oil in a skillet over medium heat and sauté onion, bell pepper, celery, and mushrooms for 5 minutes until tender. Stir in paprika and tomato paste for 1 minute. Pour in the vegetable broth and stir. Combine the remaining ingredients in a baking pan and mix in the sautéed vegetable. Bake covered with foil for 40-50 minutes.

Nutrition Info:

- Info Per Serving: Calories: 175;Fat: 8g;Protein: 5.2g;Carbs: 25.2g.

Baby Kale And Cabbage Salad

Servings:6
Cooking Time: 0 Minutes

Ingredients:

- 2 bunches baby kale, thinly sliced
- ½ head green savoy cabbage, cored and thinly sliced
- 1 medium red bell pepper, thinly sliced
- 1 garlic clove, thinly sliced
- 1 cup toasted peanuts
- Dressing:
- Juice of 1 lemon
- ¼ cup apple cider vinegar
- 1 teaspoon ground cumin
- ¼ teaspoon smoked paprika

Directions:

1. In a large mixing bowl, toss together the kale and cabbage.
2. Make the dressing: Whisk together the lemon juice, vinegar, cumin and paprika in a small bowl.
3. Pour the dressing over the greens and gently massage with your hands.
4. Add the pepper, garlic and peanuts to the mixing bowl. Toss to combine.
5. Serve immediately.

Nutrition Info:

- Info Per Serving: Calories: 199;Fat: 12.0g;Protein: 10.0g;Carbs: 17.0g.

Brussels Sprouts Linguine

Servings:4
Cooking Time: 25 Minutes

Ingredients:

- 8 ounces whole-wheat linguine
- ⅓ cup plus 2 tablespoons extra-virgin olive oil, divided
- 1 medium sweet onion, diced
- 2 to 3 garlic cloves, smashed
- 8 ounces Brussels sprouts, chopped
- ½ cup chicken stock
- ⅓ cup dry white wine
- ½ cup shredded Parmesan cheese
- 1 lemon, quartered

Directions:

1. Bring a large pot of water to a boil and cook the pasta for about 5 minutes, or until al dente. Drain the pasta and reserve 1 cup of the pasta water. Mix the cooked pasta with 2 tablespoons of the olive oil. Set aside.
2. In a large skillet, heat the remaining ⅓ cup of the olive oil over medium heat. Add the onion to the skillet and sauté for about 4 minutes, or until tender. Add the smashed garlic cloves and sauté for 1 minute, or until fragrant.
3. Stir in the Brussels sprouts and cook covered for 10 minutes. Pour in the chicken stock to prevent burning. Once the Brussels sprouts have wilted and are fork-tender, add white wine and cook for about 5 minutes, or until reduced.
4. Add the pasta to the skillet and add the pasta water as needed.
5. Top with the Parmesan cheese and squeeze the lemon over the dish right before eating.

Nutrition Info:

- Info Per Serving: Calories: 502;Fat: 31.0g;Protein: 15.0g;Carbs: 50.0g.

Chickpea Lettuce Wraps With Celery

Servings:4
Cooking Time: 0 Minutes

Ingredients:

- 1 can low-sodium chickpeas, drained and rinsed
- 1 celery stalk, thinly sliced
- 2 tablespoons finely chopped red onion
- 2 tablespoons unsalted tahini
- 3 tablespoons honey mustard
- 1 tablespoon capers, undrained
- 12 butter lettuce leaves

Directions:

1. In a bowl, mash the chickpeas with a potato masher or the back of a fork until mostly smooth.
2. Add the celery, red onion, tahini, honey mustard, and capers to the bowl and stir until well incorporated.
3. For each serving, place three overlapping lettuce leaves on a plate and top with ¼ of the mashed chickpea filling, then roll up. Repeat with the remaining lettuce leaves and chickpea mixture.

Nutrition Info:

- Info Per Serving: Calories: 182;Fat: 7.1g;Protein: 10.3g;Carbs: 19.6g.

Mini Crustless Spinach Quiches

Servings:6
Cooking Time: 20 Minutes

Ingredients:

- 2 tablespoons extra-virgin olive oil
- 1 onion, finely chopped
- 2 cups baby spinach
- 2 garlic cloves, minced
- 8 large eggs, beaten
- ¼ cup unsweetened almond milk
- ½ teaspoon sea salt
- ¼ teaspoon freshly ground black pepper
- 1 cup shredded Swiss cheese
- Cooking spray

Directions:

1. Preheat the oven to 375°F. Spritz a 6-cup muffin tin with cooking spray. Set aside.
2. In a large skillet over medium-high heat, heat the olive oil until shimmering. Add the onion and cook for about 4 minutes, or until soft. Add the spinach and cook for about 1 minute, stirring constantly, or until

the spinach softens. Add the garlic and sauté for 30 seconds. Remove from the heat and let cool.
3. In a medium bowl, whisk together the eggs, milk, salt and pepper.
4. Stir the cooled vegetables and the cheese into the egg mixture. Spoon the mixture into the prepared muffin tins. Bake for about 15 minutes, or until the eggs are set.
5. Let rest for 5 minutes before serving.

Nutrition Info:

• Info Per Serving: Calories: 218;Fat: 17.0g;Protein: 14.0g;Carbs: 4.0g.

Grilled Romaine Lettuce

Servings:4
Cooking Time: 3 To 5 Minutes

Ingredients:

- Romaine:
- 2 heads romaine lettuce, halved lengthwise
- 2 tablespoons extra-virgin olive oil
- Dressing:
- ½ cup unsweetened almond milk
- 1 tablespoon extra-virgin olive oil
- ¼ bunch fresh chives, thinly chopped
- 1 garlic clove, pressed
- 1 pinch red pepper flakes

Directions:

1. Heat a grill pan over medium heat.
2. Brush each lettuce half with the olive oil. Place the lettuce halves, flat-side down, on the grill. Grill for 3 to 5 minutes, or until the lettuce slightly wilts and develops light grill marks.
3. Meanwhile, whisk together all the ingredients for the dressing in a small bowl.
4. Drizzle 2 tablespoons of the dressing over each romaine half and serve.

Nutrition Info:

• Info Per Serving: Calories: 126;Fat: 11.0g;Protein: 2.0g;Carbs: 7.0g.

Vegetable And Red Lentil Stew

Servings:6
Cooking Time: 35 Minutes

Ingredients:

- 1 tablespoon extra-virgin olive oil
- 2 onions, peeled and finely diced
- 6½ cups water
- 2 zucchinis, finely diced
- 4 celery stalks, finely diced
- 3 cups red lentils
- 1 teaspoon dried oregano
- 1 teaspoon salt, plus more as needed

Directions:

1. Heat the olive oil in a large pot over medium heat.
2. Add the onions and sauté for about 5 minutes, stirring constantly, or until the onions are softened.
3. Stir in the water, zucchini, celery, lentils, oregano, and salt and bring the mixture to a boil.
4. Reduce the heat to low and let simmer covered for 30 minutes, stirring occasionally, or until the lentils are tender.
5. Taste and adjust the seasoning as needed.

Nutrition Info:

• Info Per Serving: Calories: 387;Fat: 4.4g;Protein: 24.0g;Carbs: 63.7g.

Sides , Salads, And Soups Recipes

Root Veggie Soup

Servings:4
Cooking Time:40 Minutes

Ingredients:

- 3 cups chopped butternut squash
- 2 tbsp olive oil
- 1 carrot, chopped
- 1 leek, chopped
- 2 garlic cloves, minced
- 1 celery stalk, chopped
- 1 parsnip, chopped
- 1 potato, chopped
- 4 cups vegetable broth
- 1 tsp dried thyme
- Salt and black pepper to taste

Directions:

1. Warm olive oil in a pot over medium heat and sauté leek, garlic, parsnip, carrot, and celery for 5-6 minutes until the veggies start to brown. Throw in squash, potato, broth, thyme, salt, and pepper. Bring to a boil, then decrease the heat and simmer for 20-30 minutes until the veggies soften. Transfer to a food processor and blend until you get a smooth and homogeneous consistency.

Nutrition Info:

- Info Per Serving: Calories: 200;Fat: 9g;Protein: 7.2g;Carbs: 25.8g.

Cucumber Salad With Goat Cheese

Servings:4
Cooking Time:15 Minutes

Ingredients:

- 2 tbsp olive oil
- 4 oz goat cheese, crumbled
- 2 cucumbers, sliced
- 2 spring onions, chopped
- 2 garlic cloves, grated
- Salt and black pepper to taste

Directions:

1. Combine cucumbers, spring onions, olive oil, garlic, salt, pepper, and goat cheese in a bowl. Serve chilled.

Nutrition Info:

- Info Per Serving: Calories: 150;Fat: 6g;Protein: 6g;-Carbs: 8g.

Anchovy Salad With Mustard Vinaigrette

Servings:6
Cooking Time:10 Minutes

Ingredients:

- ½ cup olive oil
- ½ lemon, juiced
- 1 tsp Dijon mustard
- ¼ tsp honey
- Salt and black pepper to taste
- 4 tomatoes, diced
- 1 cucumber, peeled and diced
- 1 lb arugula
- 1 red onion, thinly sliced
- 2 tbsp parsley, chopped
- 4 anchovy filets, chopped

Directions:

1. In a bowl, whisk together the olive oil, lemon juice, honey, and mustard, and season with salt and pepper. Set aside. In a separate bowl, combine all the vegetables with the parsley and toss. Add the sardine fillets on top of the salad. Drizzle the dressing over the salad just before serving.

Nutrition Info:

- Info Per Serving: Calories: 168;Fat: 6g;Protein: 8g;-Carbs: 29g.

Ritzy Summer Fruit Salad

Servings:8
Cooking Time: 0 Minutes

Ingredients:

- Salad:
- 1 cup fresh blueberries
- 2 cups cubed cantaloupe
- 2 cups red seedless grapes
- 1 cup sliced fresh strawberries
- 2 cups cubed honeydew melon
- Zest of 1 large lime
- ½ cup unsweetened toasted coconut flakes
- Dressing:
- ¼ cup raw honey
- Juice of 1 large lime
- ¼ teaspoon sea salt
- ½ cup extra-virgin olive oil

Directions:

1. Combine the ingredients for the salad in a large salad bowl, then toss to combine well.
2. Combine the ingredients for the dressing in a small bowl, then stir to mix well.
3. Dressing the salad and serve immediately.

Nutrition Info:

- Info Per Serving: Calories: 242;Fat: 15.5g;Protein: 1.3g;Carbs: 28.0g.

Parsley Carrot & Cabbage Salad

Servings:4
Cooking Time:10 Minutes

Ingredients:

- 2 tbsp olive oil
- 1 green cabbage head, torn
- 1 tbsp lemon juice
- 1 carrot, grated
- Salt and black pepper to taste
- ¼ cup parsley, chopped

Directions:

1. Mix olive oil, lemon juice, carrot, parsley, salt, pepper, and cabbage in a bowl. Serve right away.

Nutrition Info:

- Info Per Serving: Calories: 110;Fat: 5g;Protein: 5g;-Carbs: 5g.

Potato Salad

Servings:6
Cooking Time:20 Minutes

Ingredients:

- 4 russet potatoes, peeled and chopped
- 1 cup frozen mixed vegetables, thawed
- 3 hard-boiled eggs, chopped
- ½ cup Greek yogurt
- 10 pitted black olives
- ½ tsp dried mustard seeds
- ½ tsp lemon zest
- ½ tbsp lemon juice
- ½ tsp dried dill
- Salt and black pepper to taste

Directions:

1. Put the potatoes in a pot of salted water, bring to a boil, and cook for 5-7 minutes, until just fork-tender. Drain and set aside to cool. In a large bowl, mix the eggs, vegetables, yogurt, olives, pepper, mustard, lemon juice, lemon zest, and dill. Season with salt and pepper. Mix in potatoes. Serve.

Nutrition Info:

- Info Per Serving: Calories: 190;Fat: 4.8g;Protein: 9g;Carbs: 29.7g.

Carrot & Tomato Salad With Cilantro

Servings:4
Cooking Time:10 Minutes

Ingredients:

- 2 tbsp olive oil
- 4 tomatoes, chopped
- 1 carrot, grated
- ¼ cup lime juice
- 1 garlic clove, minced
- Salt and black pepper to taste
- 1 lettuce head, chopped
- 2 green onions, chopped
- ½ cup cilantro, chopped

Directions:

1. Toss lime juice, garlic, salt, pepper, olive oil, carrot, lettuce, onions, tomatoes, cilantro in a bowl. Serve cold.

Nutrition Info:

- Info Per Serving: Calories: 120;Fat: 4g;Protein: 3g;-Carbs: 4g.

Parmesan Roasted Red Potatoes

Servings:2
Cooking Time: 55 Minutes

Ingredients:

- 12 ounces red potatoes, scrubbed and diced into 1-inch pieces
- 1 tablespoon olive oil
- ½ teaspoon garlic powder
- ¼ teaspoon salt
- 1 tablespoon grated Parmesan cheese
- 1 teaspoon minced fresh rosemary

Directions:

1. Preheat the oven to 425°F. Line a baking sheet with parchment paper.
2. In a mixing bowl, combine the potatoes, olive oil, garlic powder, and salt. Toss well to coat.
3. Lay the potatoes on the parchment paper and roast for 10 minutes. Flip the potatoes over and roast for another 10 minutes.
4. Check the potatoes to make sure they are golden brown on the top and bottom. Toss them again, turn the heat down to 350°F, and roast for 30 minutes more.
5. When the potatoes are golden brown, scatter the Parmesan cheese over them and toss again. Return to the oven for 3 minutes to melt the cheese.
6. Remove from the oven and sprinkle with the fresh rosemary before serving.

Nutrition Info:

- Info Per Serving: Calories: 200;Fat: 8.2g;Protein: 5.1g;Carbs: 30.0g.

Cream Cheese Stuffed Cherry Tomatoes

Servings:6
Cooking Time:10 Minutes

Ingredients:

- 2 tbsp fresh dill, chopped
- 30 cherry tomatoes
- 3 oz cream cheese, softened
- ¼ cup mayonnaise
- 2 tbsp roasted garlic paste
- 3 tbsp grated Parmesan cheese

Directions:

1. Cut off the top of the cherry tomatoes. Discard the seeds and core with a small teaspoon. Drain upside down on paper towels. Beat the cream cheese in a small bowl until soft and fluffy. Add mayonnaise, roasted garlic paste, and Parmesan cheese; beat well. Divide the mixture between the cherry tomatoes and sprinkle with dill. Serve immediately.

Nutrition Info:

- Info Per Serving: Calories: 160;Fat: 11g;Protein: 7g;Carbs: 10g.

Mustard Chicken Salad With Avocado

Servings:4
Cooking Time:10 Minutes

Ingredients:

- 1 cup cooked chicken breasts, chopped
- ½ cup marinated artichoke hearts
- 2 tbsp olive oil
- 6 sundried tomatoes, chopped
- 1 cucumber, chopped
- 6 black olives, 6 sliced
- 2 cups Iceberg lettuce, torn
- 2 tbsp parsley, chopped
- 1 avocado, peeled and cubed
- ½ cup feta cheese, crumbled
- 4 tbsp red wine vinegar
- 2 tbsp Dijon mustard
- 1 tsp basil, dried
- 1 garlic clove, minced
- 2 tsp honey
- Salt and black pepper to taste
- 3 tbsp lemon juice

Directions:

1. Combine chicken, tomatoes, artichokes, cucumber, olives, lettuce, parsley, and avocado in a bowl. In a separate bowl, whisk vinegar, mustard, basil, garlic, honey, olive oil, salt, pepper, and lemon juice and pour over the salad. Mix well. Top with cheese and serve.

Nutrition Info:

- Info Per Serving: Calories: 340;Fat: 23g;Protein: 10g;Carbs: 26g.

Moroccan Spinach & Lentil Soup

Servings:6
Cooking Time:35 Minutes

Ingredients:

- 3 tsp olive oil
- 1 onion, chopped
- 1 large carrot, chopped
- 3 garlic cloves, sliced
- 1 ½ cups lentils
- 1 cup crushed tomatoes
- 12 oz spinach

Directions:

1. Warm the olive oil and sauté the onion, garlic, and carrot for 3 minutes. Add the lentils, tomatoes, and 6 cups of water and stir. Cook until the lentils are tender, about 15-20 minutes. Add the spinach and stir until wilted, 5 minutes. Serve hot.

Nutrition Info:

- Info Per Serving: Calories: 422;Fat: 17g;Protein: 22g;Carbs: 45g.

Bean & Shrimp Salad

Servings:4
Cooking Time:15 Minutes

Ingredients:

- 1 lb shrimp, peeled and deveined
- 30 oz canned cannellini beans, drained
- 4 tbsp olive oil
- 10 cherry tomatoes, halved
- 1 tsp lemon zest
- ½ cup red onion, chopped
- 5 oz spring mix salad
- Salt and black pepper to taste
- 2 tbsp red wine vinegar
- 2 garlic cloves, minced

Directions:

1. Warm half of the olive oil in a skillet over medium heat and cook the shrimp, turning once until just pink and opaque, about 4 minutes. Set aside to cool. Place the salad mix on a serving plate. In a bowl, mix cooled shrimp, cannellini beans, cherry tomatoes, and onion. Pour the mixture over the salad. In another bowl, whisk the remaining olive oil, red wine vinegar, garlic, lemon zest, salt, and pepper. Drizzle the dressing over the salad. Serve immediately.

Nutrition Info:

- Info Per Serving: Calories: 220;Fat: 13g;Protein: 9g;Carbs: 16g.

Balsamic Watermelon & Feta Salad

Servings:2
Cooking Time:10 Minutes

Ingredients:

- 3 cups packed arugula
- 2 ½ cups watermelon, cubed
- 2 oz feta cheese, crumbled
- 2 tbsp balsamic glaze
- 1 tsp mint leaves, chopped

Directions:

1. Place the arugula on a salad plate. Top with watermelon cubes and sprinkle with feta cheese. Drizzle the balsamic glaze all over and garnish with chopped mint leaves. Serve.

Nutrition Info:

- Info Per Serving: Calories: 159;Fat: 7.2g;Protein: 6.1g;Carbs: 21g.

Spinach & Bell Pepper Salad

Servings:4
Cooking Time:10 Minutes

Ingredients:

- 10 oz baby spinach
- 1 red bell pepper, sliced
- 2 cups corn
- 1 lemon, zested and juiced
- Salt and black pepper to taste

Directions:

1. Combine bell pepper, corn, lemon juice, lemon zest, baby spinach, salt, and pepper in a bowl. Serve immediately.

Nutrition Info:

- Info Per Serving: Calories: 190;Fat: 9g;Protein: 2g;-Carbs: 6g.

Herby Tzatziki Sauce

Servings:2
Cooking Time:10 Minutes

Ingredients:

- 1 medium cucumber, peeled and grated
- Salt to taste
- ½ cup Greek yogurt
- ½ lemon, juiced
- 1 tbsp fresh mint, chopped
- 1 tbsp fresh dill, chopped
- 1 garlic clove, minced

Directions:

1. Place the grated cucumber in a dishtowel and squeeze out the excess moisture. Transfer to a large bowl and add the lemon juice, salt, yogurt, lemon juice, mint, garlic, and dill and whisk the ingredients to combine. Store in an airtight container in the refrigerator for up to 2-3 days.

Nutrition Info:

• Info Per Serving: Calories: 179;Fat: 2.2g;Protein: 2.9g;Carbs: 7g.

Spinach & Chickpea Soup With Sausages

Servings:4
Cooking Time:35 Minutes

Ingredients:

- 2 tbsp olive oil
- 8 oz Italian sausage, sliced
- 1 can chickpeas
- 4 cups chopped spinach
- 1 onion, chopped
- 1 carrot, chopped
- 1 red bell pepper, chopped
- 3 garlic cloves, minced
- 6 cups chicken broth
- 1 tsp dried oregano
- Salt and black pepper to taste
- ½ tsp red pepper flakes

Directions:

1. Warm olive oil in a pot over medium heat. Sear the sausage for 5 minutes until browned. Set aside.
2. Add carrot, onion, garlic, and bell pepper to the pot and sauté for 5 minutes until soft. Pour in broth, chickpeas, spinach, oregano, salt, pepper, and red flakes; let simmer for 5 minutes until the spinach softens. Bring the sausage back to the pot and cook for another minute. Serve warm.

Nutrition Info:

• Info Per Serving: Calories: 473;Fat: 21g;Protein: 26g;Carbs: 47g.

Olive Tapenade Flatbread With Cheese

Servings:4
Cooking Time:35 Min + Chilling Time

Ingredients:

- For the flatbread
- 2 tbsp olive oil
- 2 ½ tsp dry yeast
- 1 ½ cups all-purpose flour
- ¾ tsp salt
- ½ cup lukewarm water
- ¼ tsp sugar
- For the tapenade
- 2 roasted red pepper slices, chopped
- ¼ cup extra-virgin olive oil
- 1 cup green olives, chopped
- 10 black olives, chopped
- 1 tbsp capers
- 1 garlic clove, minced
- 1 tbsp chopped basil leaves
- 1 tbsp chopped fresh oregano
- ¼ cup goat cheese, crumbled

Directions:

1. Combine lukewarm water, sugar, and yeast in a bowl. Set aside covered for 5 minutes. Mix the flour and salt in a bowl. Pour in the yeast mixture and mix. Knead until you obtain a ball. Place the dough onto a floured surface and knead for 5 minutes until soft. Leave the dough into an oiled bowl, covered to rise until it has doubled in size, about 40 minutes.
2. Preheat oven to 400 F. Cut the dough into 4 balls and roll each one out to a ½ inch thickness. Bake for 5 minutes. In a blender, mix black olives, roasted pepper, green olives, capers, garlic, oregano, basil, and olive oil for 20 seconds until coarsely chopped. Spread the olive tapenade on the flatbreads and top with goat cheese to serve.

Nutrition Info:

• Info Per Serving: Calories: 366;Fat: 19g;Protein: 7.3g;Carbs: 42g.

Kale & Bean Soup With Chorizo

Servings:4
Cooking Time:45 Minutes

Ingredients:

- ½ cup Manchego cheese, grated
- 1 cup canned Borlotti beans, drained
- 2 tbsp olive oil
- 1 lb Spanish chorizo, sliced
- 1 carrot, chopped
- 1 yellow onion, chopped
- 1 celery stalk, chopped
- 2 garlic cloves, minced
- ½ lb kale, chopped
- 4 cups chicken stock
- 1 tsp rosemary, dried
- Salt and black pepper to taste

Directions:

1. Warm the olive oil in a large pot over medium heat and cook the chorizo for 5 minutes or until the fat is rendered and the chorizo is browned. Add in onion and continue to cook for another 3 minutes until soft and translucent. Stir in garlic and let it cook for 30-40 seconds until fragrant. Lastly, add the carrots and celery and cook for 4-5 minutes until tender.
2. Now, pour in the chicken stock, drained and washed beans, rosemary, salt, and pepper and bring to a boil. Reduce the heat to low, cover the pot and simmer for 30 minutes. Stir periodically, checking to make sure there is enough liquid. Five minutes before the end, add the kale. Adjust the seasoning. Ladle your soup into bowls and serve topped with Manchego cheese.

Nutrition Info:

- Info Per Serving: Calories: 580;Fat: 27g;Protein: 27g;Carbs: 38g.

Pumpkin Soup With Crispy Sage Leaves

Servings:4
Cooking Time: 10 Minutes

Ingredients:

- 1 tablespoon olive oil
- 2 garlic cloves, cut into ⅛-inch-thick slices
- 1 onion, chopped
- 2 cups freshly puréed pumpkin
- 4 cups low-sodium vegetable soup
- 2 teaspoons chipotle powder
- 1 teaspoon sea salt
- ½ teaspoon freshly ground black pepper
- ½ cup vegetable oil
- 12 sage leaves, stemmed

Directions:

1. Heat the olive oil in a stockpot over high heat until shimmering.
2. Add the garlic and onion, then sauté for 5 minutes or until the onion is translucent.
3. Pour in the puréed pumpkin and vegetable soup in the pot, then sprinkle with chipotle powder, salt, and ground black pepper. Stir to mix well.
4. Bring to a boil. Reduce the heat to low and simmer for 5 minutes.
5. Meanwhile, heat the vegetable oil in a nonstick skillet over high heat.
6. Add the sage leaf to the skillet and sauté for a minute or until crispy. Transfer the sage on paper towels to soak the excess oil.
7. Gently pour the soup in three serving bowls, then divide the crispy sage leaves in bowls for garnish. Serve immediately.

Nutrition Info:

- Info Per Serving: Calories: 380;Fat: 20.1g;Protein: 8.9g;Carbs: 45.2g.

Neapolitan Pasta & Fagioli

Servings:4
Cooking Time:60 Minutes

Ingredients:

- ½ cup canned red kidney beans, drained
- 1 tbsp olive oil
- 1 carrot, diced
- 1 celery stalk, diced
- 1 onion, diced
- 1 large garlic clove, minced
- 2 tsp tomato paste
- 4 cups vegetable broth
- 1 cup kale, chopped
- ½ cup elbow macaroni
- 2 tbsp fresh basil, chopped
- Salt and black pepper to taste

Directions:

1. Warm the olive oil in a stockpot over medium heat. Add the carrot, celery, onion, and garlic and sauté for 5 minutes or until the vegetables start to turn golden. Stir in the tomato paste and cook for about 30 seconds.

Add the vegetable broth, beans, and elbow macaroni and bring to a boil. Simmer for 8-10 minutes. Add the kale and cook for 4-5 minutes. Adjust the seasoning with salt and pepper. Serve topped with basil. Enjoy!

Nutrition Info:

- Info Per Serving: Calories: 215;Fat: 4.2g;Protein: 11g;Carbs: 36g.

Kale & Chicken Soup With Vermicelli

Servings:4
Cooking Time:25 Minutes

Ingredients:

- 2 tbsp olive oil
- 1 carrot, chopped
- 1 leek, chopped
- ½ cup vermicelli
- 4 cups chicken stock
- 2 cups kale, chopped
- 2 chicken breasts, cubed
- 1 cup orzo
- ¼ cup lemon juice
- 2 tbsp parsley, chopped
- Salt and black pepper to taste

Directions:

1. Warm the olive oil in a pot over medium heat and sauté leek and chicken for 6 minutes. Stir in carrot and chicken stock and bring to a boil. Cook for 10 minutes. Add in vermicelli, kale, orzo, and lemon juice and continue cooking for another 5 minutes. Adjust the seasoning with salt and pepper and sprinkle with parsley. Ladle into soup bowls and serve.

Nutrition Info:

- Info Per Serving: Calories: 310;Fat: 13g;Protein: 13g;Carbs: 17g.

Parsley Garden Vegetable Soup

Servings:4
Cooking Time:25 Minutes

Ingredients:

- ¼ head green cabbage, shredded
- 2 tbsp olive oil
- 1 cup leeks, chopped
- 2 garlic cloves, minced
- 8 cups vegetable stock
- 1 carrot, diced
- 1 potato, diced
- 1 celery stalk, diced
- 1 cup mushrooms
- 1 cup broccoli florets
- 1 cup cauliflower florets
- ½ red bell pepper, diced
- ½ cup green beans
- Salt and black pepper to taste
- 2 tbsp fresh parsley, chopped

Directions:

1. Heat oil on Sauté in your Instant Pot. Add in garlic and leeks and cook for 6 minutes until slightly browned. Add in stock, carrot, celery, broccoli, bell pepper, green beans, salt, cabbage, cauliflower, mushrooms, potato, and pepper. Seal lid and cook on High Pressure for 6 minutes. Release pressure naturally for about 10 minutes. Stir in parsley and serve.

Nutrition Info:

- Info Per Serving: Calories: 218;Fat: 7g;Protein: 5g;-Carbs: 36g.

Roasted Cherry Tomato & Fennel

Servings:4
Cooking Time:35 Minutes

Ingredients:

- ¼ cup olive oil
- 20 cherry tomatoes, halved
- 2 fennel bulbs, cut into wedges
- 10 black olives, sliced
- 1 lemon, cut into wedges
- Salt and black pepper to taste

Directions:

1. Preheat oven to 425 F. Combine fennel, olive oil, tomatoes, salt, and pepper in a bowl. Place in a baking pan and roast in the oven for about 25 minutes until golden. Top with olives and serve with lemon wedges on the side.

Nutrition Info:

- Info Per Serving: Calories: 268;Fat: 15.2g;Protein: 7g;Carbs: 33g.

Green Bean & Rice Chicken Soup

Servings:4
Cooking Time:45 Minutes

Ingredients:

- 2 tbsp olive oil
- 4 cups chicken stock
- ½ lb chicken breasts strips
- 1 celery stalk, chopped
- 2 garlic cloves, minced
- 1 yellow onion, chopped
- ½ cup white rice
- 1 egg, whisked
- ½ lemon, juiced
- 1 cup green beans, chopped
- 1 cup carrots, chopped
- ½ cup dill, chopped
- Salt and black pepper to taste

Directions:

1. Warm the olive oil in a pot over medium heat and sauté onion, garlic, celery, carrots, and chicken for 6-7 minutes.
2. Pour in stock and rice. Bring to a boil and simmer for 10 minutes. Stir in green beans, salt, and pepper and cook for 15 minutes. Whisk the egg and lemon juice and pour into the pot. Stir and cook for 2 minutes. Serve topped with dill.

Nutrition Info:

- Info Per Serving: Calories: 270;Fat: 19g;Protein: 15g;Carbs: 20g.

Spinach & Pea Salad With Rice

Servings:2
Cooking Time:30 Minutes

Ingredients:

- 1 tbsp olive oil
- Salt and black pepper to taste
- ½ cup baby spinach
- ½ cup green peas, blanched
- 1 garlic clove, minced
- ½ cup white rice, rinsed
- 6 cherry tomatoes, halved
- 1 tbsp parsley, chopped
- 2 tbsp Italian salad dressing

Directions:

1. Bring a large pot of salted water to a boil over medium heat. Pour in the rice, cover, and simmer on low heat for 15-18 minutes or until the rice is al dente. Drain and let cool.
2. In a bowl, whisk the olive oil, garlic, salt, and black pepper. Toss the green peas, baby spinach, and rice together. Pour the dressing all over and gently stir to combine. Decorate with cherry tomatoes and parsley and serve. Enjoy!

Nutrition Info:

- Info Per Serving: Calories: 160;Fat: 14g;Protein: 4g;Carbs: 9g.

Octopus, Calamari & Watercress Salad

Servings:4
Cooking Time:50 Minutes

Ingredients:

- 2 tbsp olive oil
- 2 cups olives, sliced
- 1 octopus, tentacles separated
- 2 oz calamari rings
- 3 garlic cloves, minced
- 1 white onion, chopped
- ¾ cup chicken stock
- 2 cups watercress, sliced
- 1 cup parsley, chopped
- Salt and black pepper to taste
- 1 tbsp red wine vinegar

Directions:

1. Place octopus, stock, calamari rings, salt, and pepper in a pot over medium heat and bring to a simmer. Cook for 40 minutes. Strain seafood and let cool completely. Chop tentacles into pieces. Remove to a serving bowl along with the calamari rings. Stir in garlic, onion, watercress, olives, parsley, red wine vinegar, and olive oil and toss to coat.

Nutrition Info:

- Info Per Serving: Calories: 300;Fat: 11g;Protein: 9g;Carbs: 23g.

Simple Green Salad

Servings:4
Cooking Time:10 Minutes

Ingredients:

- 2 tbsp olive oil
- 10 cherry tomatoes, halved
- 2 cucumbers, sliced
- 1 romaine lettuce head, torn
- 2 tbsp parsley, chopped
- 1 lemon, juiced

Directions:

1. Combine olive oil, cucumbers, lettuce, tomatoes, parsley, and lemon juice in a bowl. Serve chilled.

Nutrition Info:

- Info Per Serving: Calories: 150;Fat: 6g;Protein: 5g;-Carbs: 2g.

Creamy Tomato Hummus Soup

Servings:4
Cooking Time:10 Minutes

Ingredients:

- 1 can diced tomatoes
- 1 cup traditional hummus
- 4 cups chicken stock
- ¼ cup basil leaves, sliced
- 1 cup garlic croutons

Directions:

1. Place the tomatoes, hummus, and chicken stock in your blender and blend until smooth. Pour the mixture into a saucepan over medium heat and bring it to a boil. Pour the soup into bowls. Sprinkle with basil and serve with croutons.

Nutrition Info:

- Info Per Serving: Calories: 148;Fat: 6.2g;Protein: 5g;Carbs: 18.8g.

Authentic Chicken Soup With Vegetables

Servings:4
Cooking Time:35 Minutes

Ingredients:

- 2 tsp olive oil
- 1 cup mushrooms, chopped
- 1 large carrot, chopped
- 1 yellow onion, chopped
- 1 celery stalk, chopped
- 2 yellow squash, chopped
- 2 chicken breasts, cubed
- ½ cup chopped fresh parsley
- 4 cups chicken stock
- Salt and black pepper to taste

Directions:

1. Warm the oil in a skillet over medium heat. Place in carrot, onion, mushrooms, and celery and cook for 5 minutes. Stir in chicken and cook for 10 more minutes. Mix in squash, salt, and black pepper. Cook for 5 minutes, then lower the heat and pour in the stock. Cook covered for 10 more minutes. Divide between bowls and scatter with parsley.

Nutrition Info:

- Info Per Serving: Calories: 335;Fat: 9g;Protein: 33g;Carbs: 28g.

Warm Kale Salad With Red Bell Pepper

Servings:4
Cooking Time:15 Minutes

Ingredients:

- 1 tbsp olive oil
- 4 cups kale, torn
- 2 cloves garlic, minced
- 1 red bell pepper, diced
- Salt and black pepper to taste
- ½ lemon, juiced

Directions:

1. Warm the olive oil in a large skillet over medium heat and add the garlic. Cook for 1 minute, and then add the bell pepper. Cook for 4-5 minutes until the pepper is tender. Stir in the kale. Cook for 3-4 minutes or just until wilted, then remove from heat. Place pepper and kale in a bowl and season with salt and black pepper. Drizzle with lemon juice.

Nutrition Info:

- Info Per Serving: Calories: 123;Fat: 4g;Protein: 6g;-Carbs: 22g.

Poultry And Meats Recipes

Picante Beef Stew

Servings:4
Cooking Time:35 Minutes

Ingredients:

- 2 tbsp olive oil
- 1 carrot, chopped
- 4 potatoes, diced
- 1 tsp ground nutmeg
- ½ tsp cinnamon
- 1 lb beef stew meat, cubed
- ½ cup sweet chili sauce
- ½ cup vegetable stock
- 1 tbsp cilantro, chopped
- Salt and black pepper to taste

Directions:

1. Warm the olive oil in a skillet over medium heat and sear beef for 5 minutes. Stir in chili sauce, carrot, potatoes, stock, nutmeg, cinnamon, cilantro, salt, and pepper and bring to a boil. Cook for another 20 minutes. Serve immediately.

Nutrition Info:

- Info Per Serving: Calories: 300;Fat: 22g;Protein: 20g;Carbs: 26g.

Harissa Turkey With Couscous

Servings:4
Cooking Time:20 Min + Marinating Time

Ingredients:

- 1 lb skinless turkey breast slices
- 2 tbsp olive oil
- 1 tsp garlic powder
- ½ tsp ground coriander
- 1 tbsp harissa seasoning
- 1 cup couscous
- 2 tbsp raisins, soaked
- 2 tbsp chopped parsley
- Salt and black pepper to taste

Directions:

1. Whisk the olive oil, garlic powder, ground coriander, harissa, salt, and pepper in a bowl. Add the turkey slices and toss to coat. Marinate covered for 30 minutes. Place the couscous in a large bowl and pour 1 ½ cups of salted boiling water. Cover and leave to sit for 5 minutes. Fluff with a fork and stir in raisins and parsley. Keep warm until ready to serve.
2. Preheat your grill to high. Place the turkey slices on the grill and cook for 3 minutes per side until cooked through with no pink showing. Serve with the couscous.

Nutrition Info:

- Info Per Serving: Calories: 350;Fat: 7g;Protein: 47g;Carbs: 19g.

Beef Stuffed Peppers

Servings:4
Cooking Time:50 Minutes

Ingredients:

- 2 tbsp olive oil
- 2 red bell peppers
- 1 lb ground beef
- 1 shallot, finely chopped
- 2 garlic cloves, minced
- 2 tbsp fresh sage, chopped
- Salt and black pepper to taste
- 1 tsp ground allspice
- ½ cup fresh parsley, chopped
- ½ cup baby arugula leaves
- ½ cup pine nuts, chopped
- 1 tbsp orange juice

Directions:

1. Warm the olive oil in a large skillet over medium heat. Sauté the beef, garlic, and shallot for 8-10 minutes until the meat is browned and cooked through. Season with sage, allspice, salt, and pepper and remove from the heat to cool slightly. Stir in parsley, arugula, pine nuts, and orange juice and mix.
2. Preheat oven to 390 F. Slice the peppers in half lengthwise and remove the seeds and membranes. Spoon the filling into the pepper halves. Bake the oven for 25-30 minutes.

Nutrition Info:

- Info Per Serving: Calories: 521;Fat: 44g;Protein: 25g;Carbs: 9g.

Chicken & Spinach Dish

Servings:4
Cooking Time:60 Minutes

Ingredients:

- 2 tbsp olive oil
- 2 cups baby spinach
- 1 lb chicken sausage, sliced
- 1 red bell pepper, chopped
- 1 onion, sliced
- 2 tbsp garlic, minced
- Salt and black pepper to taste
- ½ cup chicken stock
- 1 tbsp balsamic vinegar

Directions:

1. Preheat oven to 380 F. Warm olive oil in a skillet over medium heat. Cook sausages for 6 minutes on all sides. Remove to a bowl. Add the bell pepper, onion, garlic, salt, pepper to the skillet and sauté for 5 minutes. Pour in stock and vinegar and return the sausages. Bring to a boil and cook for 10 minutes. Add in the spinach and cook until wilts, about 4 minutes. Serve and enjoy!

Nutrition Info:

- Info Per Serving: Calories: 300;Fat: 15g;Protein: 27g;Carbs: 18g.

Slow Cooker Beef Stew

Servings:4
Cooking Time:8 Hours 10 Minutes

Ingredients:

- 2 tbsp canola oil
- 2 lb beef stew meat, cubed
- Salt and black pepper to taste
- 2 cups beef stock
- 2 shallots, chopped
- 2 tbsp thyme, chopped
- 2 garlic cloves, minced
- 1 carrot, chopped
- 3 celery stalks, chopped
- 28 oz canned tomatoes, diced
- 2 tbsp parsley, chopped

Directions:

1. Place the beef meat, salt, pepper, beef stock, canola oil, shallots, thyme, garlic, carrot, celery, and tomatoes in your slow cooker. Put the lid and cook for 8 hours on Low. Sprinkle with parsley and serve warm.

Nutrition Info:

- Info Per Serving: Calories: 370;Fat: 17g;Protein: 35g;Carbs: 28g.

Cocktail Meatballs In Almond Sauce

Servings:4
Cooking Time:30 Minutes

Ingredients:

- 3 tbsp olive oil
- 8 oz ground pork
- 8 oz ground beef
- ½ cup finely minced onions
- 1 large egg, beaten
- 1 potato, shredded
- Salt and black pepper to taste
- 1 tsp garlic powder
- ½ tsp oregano
- 2 tbsp chopped parsley
- ¼ cup ground almonds
- 1 cup chicken broth
- ¼ cup butter

Directions:

1. Place the ground meat, onions, egg, potato, salt, garlic powder, pepper, and oregano in a large bowl. Shape the mixture into small meatballs, about 1 inch in diameter, and place on a plate. Let sit for 10 minutes at room temperature.
2. Warm the olive oil in a skillet over medium heat. Add the meatballs and brown them for 6-8 minutes on all sides; reserve. In the hot skillet, melt the butter and add the almonds and broth. Cook for 3-5 minutes. Add the meatballs to the skillet, cover, and cook for 8-10 minutes. Top with parsley.

Nutrition Info:

- Info Per Serving: Calories: 449;Fat: 42g;Protein: 16g;Carbs: 3g.

~~Vegetable & Turkey Traybake~~

Servings:4
Cooking Time:80 Minutes

Ingredients:

- 2 tbsp olive oil
- 1 lb turkey breast, cubed
- 1 head broccoli, cut into florets
- 2 oz cherry tomatoes, halved
- 2 tbsp cilantro, chopped
- 1 lemon, zested
- Salt and black pepper to taste
- 2 spring onions, chopped

Directions:

1. Preheat the oven to 360 F. Warm the olive oil in a skillet over medium heat and sauté spring onions and lemon zest for 3 minutes. Add in turkey and cook for another 5-6 minutes, stirring occasionally. Transfer to a baking dish, pour in 1 cup of water and bake for 30 minutes. Add in broccoli and tomatoes and bake for another 10 minutes. Top with cilantro.

Nutrition Info:

- Info Per Serving: Calories: 310;Fat: 10g;Protein: 15g;Carbs: 21g.

~~Eggplant & Chicken Skillet~~

Servings:4
Cooking Time:40 Minutes

Ingredients:

- 2 tbsp olive oil
- 1 lb eggplants, cubed
- Salt and black pepper to taste
- 1 onion, chopped
- 2 garlic cloves, minced
- 1 tsp hot paprika
- 1 tbsp oregano, chopped
- 1 cup chicken stock
- 1 lb chicken breasts, cubed
- 1 cup half and half
- 3 tsp toasted chopped almonds

Directions:

1. Warm the olive oil in a skillet over medium heat and sauté chicken for 8 minutes, stirring often. Mix in eggplants, onion, and garlic and cook for another 5 minutes. Season with salt, pepper, hot paprika, and oregano and pour in the stock. Bring to a boil and simmer for 16 minutes. Stir in half and half for 2 minutes. Serve topped with almonds.

Nutrition Info:

- Info Per Serving: Calories: 400;Fat: 13g;Protein: 26g;Carbs: 22g.

Grilled Chicken And Zucchini Kebabs

Servings:4
Cooking Time: 20 Minutes

Ingredients:

- ¼ cup extra-virgin olive oil
- 2 tablespoons balsamic vinegar
- 1 teaspoon dried oregano, crushed between your fingers
- 1 pound boneless, skinless chicken breasts, cut into 1½-inch pieces
- 2 medium zucchinis, cut into 1-inch pieces
- ½ cup Kalamata olives, pitted and halved
- 2 tablespoons olive brine
- ¼ cup torn fresh basil leaves
- Nonstick cooking spray
- Special Equipment:
- 14 to 15 wooden skewers, soaked for at least 30 minutes

Directions:

1. Spray the grill grates with nonstick cooking spray. Preheat the grill to medium-high heat.
2. In a small bowl, whisk together the olive oil, vinegar, and oregano. Divide the marinade between two large plastic zip-top bags.
3. Add the chicken to one bag and the zucchini to another. Seal and massage the marinade into both the chicken and zucchini.
4. Thread the chicken onto 6 wooden skewers. Thread the zucchini onto 8 or 9 wooden skewers.
5. Cook the kebabs in batches on the grill for 5 minutes, flip, and grill for 5 minutes more, or until any chicken juices run clear.
6. Remove the chicken and zucchini from the skewers to a large serving bowl. Toss with the olives, olive brine, and basil and serve.

Nutrition Info:

- Info Per Serving: Calories: 283;Fat: 15.0g;Protein: 11.0g;Carbs: 26.0g.

Creamy Chicken Balls With Almonds

Servings:4
Cooking Time:30 Minutes

Ingredients:

- 2 tbsp olive oil
- 1 lb ground chicken
- 2 tsp toasted chopped almonds
- 1 egg, whisked
- 2 tsp turmeric powder
- 2 garlic cloves, minced
- Salt and black pepper to taste
- 1 ¼ cups heavy cream
- ¼ cup parsley, chopped
- 1 tbsp chives, chopped

Directions:

1. Place chicken, almonds, egg, turmeric powder, garlic, salt, pepper, parsley, and chives in a bowl and toss to combine. Form meatballs out of the mixture. Warm olive oil in a skillet over medium heat. Brown meatballs for 8 minutes on all sides. Stir in cream and cook for another 10 minutes.

Nutrition Info:

- Info Per Serving: Calories: 290;Fat: 10g;Protein: 36g;Carbs: 26g.

Easy Pork Stew

Servings:4
Cooking Time:50 Minutes

Ingredients:

- 1 tbsp olive oil
- 1 lb pork stew meat, cubed
- 2 shallots, chopped
- 14 oz canned tomatoes, diced
- 1 garlic clove, minced
- 3 cups beef stock
- 2 tbsp paprika
- 1 tsp coriander seeds
- 1 tsp dried thyme
- Salt and black pepper to taste
- 2 tbsp parsley, chopped

Directions:

1. Warm the olive oil in a pot over medium heat and cook pork meat for 5 minutes until brown, stirring occasionally. Add in shallots and garlic and cook for an additional 3 minutes. Stir in beef stock, tomatoes, paprika, thyme, coriander seeds, salt, and pepper and bring to a boil; cook for 30 minutes. Serve warm topped with parsley.

Nutrition Info:

- Info Per Serving: Calories: 330;Fat: 18g;Protein: 35g;Carbs: 28g.

Peppery Chicken Bake

Servings:4
Cooking Time:70 Minutes

Ingredients:

- 3 tbsp olive oil
- 1 lb chicken breasts, sliced
- 2 lb cherry tomatoes, halved
- 1 onion, chopped
- 3 garlic cloves, minced
- 3 red chili peppers, chopped
- ½ lemon, zested
- Salt and black pepper to taste

Directions:

1. Warm the olive oil in a skillet over medium heat and brown chicken for 8 minutes on both sides. Remove to a roasting pan. In the same skillet, add onion, garlic, and chili peppers and cook for 2 minutes. Pour the mixture over the chicken and toss to coat. Add in tomatoes, lemon zest, 1 cup of water, salt, and pepper. Bake for 45 minutes. Serve and enjoy!

Nutrition Info:

- Info Per Serving: Calories: 280;Fat: 14g;Protein: 34g;Carbs: 25g.

Potato Lamb And Olive Stew

Servings:10
Cooking Time: 3 Hours 42 Minutes

Ingredients:

- 4 tablespoons almond flour
- ¾ cup low-sodium chicken stock
- 1¼ pounds small potatoes, halved
- 3 cloves garlic, minced
- 4 large shallots, cut into ½-inch wedges
- 3 sprigs fresh rosemary
- 1 tablespoon lemon zest
- Coarse sea salt and black pepper, to taste
- 3½ pounds lamb shanks, fat trimmed and cut crosswise into 1½-inch pieces
- 2 tablespoons extra-virgin olive oil
- ½ cup dry white wine
- 1 cup pitted green olives, halved
- 2 tablespoons lemon juice

Directions:

1. Combine 1 tablespoon of almond flour with chicken stock in a bowl. Stir to mix well.
2. Put the flour mixture, potatoes, garlic, shallots, rosemary, and lemon zest in the slow cooker. Sprinkle with salt and black pepper. Stir to mix well. Set aside.
3. Combine the remaining almond flour with salt and black pepper in a large bowl, then dunk the lamb shanks in the flour and toss to coat.
4. Heat the olive oil in a nonstick skillet over medium-high heat until shimmering.
5. Add the well-coated lamb and cook for 10 minutes or until golden brown. Flip the lamb pieces halfway through the cooking time. Transfer the cooked lamb to the slow cooker.
6. Pour the wine in the same skillet, then cook for 2 minutes or until it reduces in half. Pour the wine in the slow cooker.
7. Put the slow cooker lid on and cook on high for 3 hours and 30 minutes or until the lamb is very tender.
8. In the last 20 minutes of the cooking, open the lid and fold in the olive halves to cook.
9. Pour the stew on a large plate, let them sit for 5 minutes, then skim any fat remains over the face of the liquid.
10. Drizzle with lemon juice and sprinkle with salt and pepper. Serve warm.

Nutrition Info:

- Info Per Serving: Calories: 309;Fat: 10.3g;Protein: 36.9g;Carbs: 16.1g.

Thyme Chicken Roast

Servings:4
Cooking Time:65 Minutes

Ingredients:

- 1 tbsp butter, softened
- 1 lb chicken drumsticks
- 2 garlic cloves, minced
- 1 tsp paprika
- 1 lemon, zested
- 1 tbsp chopped fresh thyme
- Salt and black pepper to taste

Directions:

1. Preheat oven to 350 F. Mix butter, thyme, paprika, salt, garlic, pepper, and lemon zest in a bowl. Rub the mixture all over the chicken drumsticks and arrange them on a baking dish. Add in ½ cup of water and roast in the oven for 50-60 minutes. Remove the chicken from the oven and let it sit covered with foil for 10 minutes. Serve and enjoy!

Nutrition Info:

- Info Per Serving: Calories: 219;Fat: 9.4g;Protein: 31g;Carbs: 0.5g.

Date Lamb Tangine

Servings:4
Cooking Time:40 Minutes

Ingredients:

- 2 tbsp olive oil
- 1 tbsp dates, chopped
- 1 lb lamb, cubed
- 1 garlic clove, minced
- 1 onion, grated
- 2 tbsp orange juice
- Salt and black pepper to taste
- 1 cup vegetable stock

Directions:

1. Warm the olive oil in a skillet over medium heat and cook onion and garlic for 5 minutes. Put in lamb and cook for another 5 minutes. Stir in dates, orange juice, salt, pepper, and stock and bring to a boil; cook for 20 minutes. Serve.

Nutrition Info:

- Info Per Serving: Calories: 298;Fat: 14g;Protein: 17g;Carbs: 19g.

Greek-style Chicken & Egg Bake

Servings:4
Cooking Time:45 Minutes

Ingredients:

- ½ lb Halloumi cheese, grated
- 1 tbsp olive oil
- 1 lb chicken breasts, cubed
- 4 eggs, beaten
- 1 tsp dry mustard
- 2 cloves garlic, crushed
- 2 red bell peppers, sliced
- 1 red onion, sliced
- 2 tomatoes, chopped
- 1 tsp sweet paprika
- ½ tsp dried basil
- Salt to taste

Directions:

1. Preheat oven to 360 F. Warm the olive oil in a skillet over medium heat. Add the bell peppers, garlic, onion, and salt and cook for 3 minutes. Stir in tomatoes for an additional 5 minutes. Put in chicken breasts, paprika, dry mustard, and basil. Cook for another 6-8 minutes. Transfer the mixture to a greased baking pan and pour over the beaten eggs; season with salt. Bake for 15-18 minutes. Remove and spread the cheese over the top. Let cool for a few minutes. Serve sliced.

Nutrition Info:

• Info Per Serving: Calories: 480;Fat: 31g;Protein: 39g;Carbs: 12g.

Quinoa & Chicken Bowl

Servings:4
Cooking Time:50 Minutes

Ingredients:

- 4 chicken things, skinless and boneless
- 2 tbsp olive oil
- Salt and black pepper to taste
- 1 celery stalk, chopped
- 2 leeks, chopped
- 2 cups chicken stock
- 2 tbsp cilantro, chopped
- 1 cup quinoa
- 1 tsp lemon zest

Directions:

1. Warm the olive oil in a pot over medium heat and cook the chicken for 6-8 minutes on all sides. Stir in leeks and celery and cook for another 5 minutes until tender. Season with salt and pepper. Stir in quinoa and lemon zest for 1 minute and pour in the chicken stock. Bring to a boil and simmer for 35 minutes. Serve topped with cilantro.

Nutrition Info:

• Info Per Serving: Calories: 250;Fat: 14g;Protein: 35g;Carbs: 17g.

Almond-crusted Chicken Tenders With Honey

Servings:4
Cooking Time: 20 Minutes

Ingredients:

- 1 tablespoon honey
- 1 tablespoon whole-grain or Dijon mustard
- ¼ teaspoon freshly ground black pepper
- ¼ teaspoon kosher or sea salt
- 1 pound boneless, skinless chicken breast tenders or tenderloins
- 1 cup almonds, roughly chopped
- Nonstick cooking spray

Directions:

1. Preheat the oven to 425°F. Line a large, rimmed baking sheet with parchment paper. Place a wire cooling rack on the parchment-lined baking sheet, and spray the rack well with nonstick cooking spray.
2. In a large bowl, combine the honey, mustard, pepper, and salt. Add the chicken and toss gently to coat. Set aside.
3. Dump the almonds onto a large sheet of parchment paper and spread them out. Press the coated chicken tenders into the nuts until evenly coated on all sides. Place the chicken on the prepared wire rack.
4. Bake in the preheated oven for 15 to 20 minutes, or until the internal temperature of the chicken measures 165°F on a meat thermometer and any juices run clear.
5. Cool for 5 minutes before serving.

Nutrition Info:

• Info Per Serving: Calories: 222;Fat: 7.0g;Protein: 11.0g;Carbs: 29.0g.

Italian-style Chianti Pork Tenderloin

Servings:4
Cooking Time:30 Minutes

Ingredients:

- ½ cup Chianti red wine
- 1 tsp Mediterranean seasoning
- 1 cup red onions, chopped
- 2 garlic cloves, minced
- 1 Italian pepper, chopped
- 2 tbsp olive oil
- 1 tbsp Dijon mustard
- 1 ½ lb pork tenderloin

Directions:

1. Rub the tenderloin steak with mustard and Mediterranean seasoning. Heat the olive oil in a skillet over medium heat. Cook the tenderloin steak for 9-10 minutes per side. Sauté the onion, garlic, and Italian pepper for 3 to 4 minutes more until they've softened. Add in red wine to scrape up any browned bits from the bottom of the skillet. Continue to cook until the cooking liquid has thickened and reduced by half. Slice the tenderloin and serve topped with the sauce.

Nutrition Info:

- Info Per Serving: Calories: 450;Fat: 34g;Protein: 34g;Carbs: 4g.

Fennel Beef Ribs

Servings:4
Cooking Time:2 Hours 10 Minutes

Ingredients:

- 2 tbsp olive oil
- 2 lb beef ribs
- 2 garlic cloves, minced
- 1 onion, chopped
- ½ cup chicken stock
- 1 tbsp ground fennel seeds

Directions:

1. Preheat oven to 360 F. Mix garlic, onion, stock, olive oil, fennel seeds, and beef ribs in a roasting pan and bake for 2 hours. Serve hot with salad.

Nutrition Info:

- Info Per Serving: Calories: 300;Fat: 10g;Protein: 25g;Carbs: 18g.

Chicken Lentils With Artichokes

Servings:4
Cooking Time:50 Minutes

Ingredients:

- 2 tbsp olive oil
- 4 chicken breasts, halved
- 1 lemon, juiced and zested
- 2 garlic cloves, crushed
- 1 tbsp thyme, chopped
- 6 oz canned artichokes hearts
- 1 cup canned lentils, drained
- 1 cup chicken stock
- 1 tsp cayenne pepper
- Salt and black pepper to taste

Directions:

1. Warm the olive oil in a skillet over medium heat and cook chicken for 5-6 minutes until browned, flipping once. Mix in lemon zest, garlic, lemon juice, salt, pepper, thyme, artichokes, lentils, stock, and cayenne pepper and bring to a boil. Cook for 35 minutes. Serve immediately.

Nutrition Info:

- Info Per Serving: Calories: 300;Fat: 16g;Protein: 25g;Carbs: 25g.

Sausage & Herb Eggs

Servings:2
Cooking Time:20 Minutes

Ingredients:

- 2 tbsp olive oil
- ½ cup leeks, chopped
- ½ lb pork sausage, crumbled
- 4 eggs, whisked
- 1 thyme sprig, chopped
- 1 tsp habanero pepper, minced
- ½ tsp dried marjoram
- 1 tsp garlic puree
- ½ cup green olives, sliced
- Salt and black pepper to taste

Directions:

1. Warm the olive oil in a skillet over medium heat. Sauté the leeks until they are just tender, about 4 minutes. Add the garlic, habanero pepper, salt, black pepper, and sausage; cook for 8 minutes, stirring frequently. Pour in the eggs and sprinkle with thyme and

marjoram. Cook for an additional 4 minutes, stirring with a spoon. Garnish with olives. Serve.

Nutrition Info:

- Info Per Serving: Calories: 460;Fat: 41g;Protein: 16g;Carbs: 6g.

French Chicken Cassoulet

Servings:4
Cooking Time:40 Minutes

Ingredients:

- 1 tbsp olive oil
- ½ cup heavy cream
- 4 chicken breasts, halved
- 1/3 cup yellow mustard
- Salt and black pepper to taste
- 1 onion, chopped
- 1 ½ cups chicken stock
- ¼ tsp dried oregano

Directions:

1. Warm stock in a saucepan over medium heat and stir in mustard, onion, salt, pepper, and oregano. Bring to a boil and cook for 8 minutes. Warm olive oil in a skillet over medium heat. Sear chicken for 6 minutes on both sides. Transfer to the saucepan and simmer for another 12 minutes. Stir in heavy cream for 2 minutes. Serve warm.

Nutrition Info:

- Info Per Serving: Calories: 260;Fat: 12g;Protein: 27g;Carbs: 18g.

Smooth Chicken Breasts With Nuts

Servings:4
Cooking Time:40 Minutes

Ingredients:

- 2 tbsp olive oil
- 1 ½ lb chicken breasts, cubed
- 4 spring onions, chopped
- 2 carrots, peeled and sliced
- ¼ cup mayonnaise
- ½ cup Greek yogurt
- 1 cup toasted cashews, chopped
- Salt and black pepper to taste

Directions:

1. Warm the olive oil in a skillet over medium heat and brown chicken for 8 minutes on all sides. Stir in spring onions, carrots, mayonnaise, yogurt, salt, and pepper and bring to a simmer. Cook for 20 minutes. Top with cashews to serve.

Nutrition Info:

- Info Per Serving: Calories: 310;Fat: 15g;Protein: 16g;Carbs: 20g.

Roasted Herby Chicken

Servings:4
Cooking Time:80 Minutes

Ingredients:

- 2 tbsp butter, melted
- 1 chicken
- 2 lemons, halved
- 4 rosemary sprigs
- 1 bay leaf
- 6 thyme sprigs
- 1 tsp lemon juice
- Salt and black pepper to taste

Directions:

1. Preheat oven to 420 F and fit a rack into a roasting tray. Brush the chicken with butter on all sides. Put the lemons, herbs, and bay leaf inside the cavity. Drizzle with lemon juice and sprinkle with salt and pepper. Roast for 60-65 minutes. Let rest for 10 minutes before carving.

Nutrition Info:

- Info Per Serving: Calories: 235;Fat: 7g;Protein: 32g;Carbs: 2g.

Hot Pork Meatballs

Servings:4
Cooking Time:30 Minutes

Ingredients:

- 3 tbsp olive oil
- 1 lb ground pork
- 2 tbsp parsley, chopped
- 2 green onions, chopped
- 4 garlic cloves, minced
- 1 red chili, chopped
- 1 cup veggie stock
- 2 tbsp hot paprika

Directions:

1. Combine pork, parsley, green onions, garlic, and red chili in a bowl and form medium balls out of the mixture. Warm olive oil in a skillet over medium heat. Sear meatballs for 8 minutes on all sides. Stir in stock and hot paprika and simmer for another 12 minutes. Serve warm.

Nutrition Info:

• Info Per Serving: Calories: 240;Fat: 19g;Protein: 15g;Carbs: 12g.

Mustardy Turkey Ham Stuffed Peppers

Servings:4
Cooking Time:10 Minutes

Ingredients:

- 1 cup Greek yogurt
- 1 lb turkey ham, chopped
- 2 tbsp mustard
- Salt and black pepper to taste
- 1 celery stalk, chopped
- 2 tbsp balsamic vinegar
- 1 bunch scallions, sliced
- ¼ cup parsley, chopped
- 1 cucumber, sliced
- 1 red bell peppers, halved and deseeded
- 1 tomato, sliced

Directions:

1. Preheat the oven to 360 F. Combine turkey ham, celery, balsamic vinegar, salt, pepper, mustard, yogurt, scallions, parsley, cucumber, and tomatoes in a bowl. Fill bell peppers with the mixture and arrange them on a greased baking dish. Bake in the oven for about 20 minutes. Serve warm.

Nutrition Info:

• Info Per Serving: Calories: 280;Fat: 13g;Protein: 4g;Carbs: 16g.

Chicken Pappardelle With Mushrooms

Servings:2
Cooking Time:30 Minutes

Ingredients:

- 4 oz cremini mushrooms, sliced
- 2 tbsp olive oil
- ½ onion, minced
- 2 garlic cloves, minced
- 8 oz chicken breasts, cubed
- 2 tsp tomato paste
- 2 tsp dried tarragon
- 2 cups chicken stock
- 6 oz pappardelle pasta
- ¼ cup Greek yogurt
- Salt and black pepper to taste
- ¼ tsp red pepper flakes

Directions:

1. Warm 1 tablespoon of olive oil in a pan over medium heat. Suté the onion, garlic, and mushrooms for 5 minutes. Move the vegetables to the edges of the pan and add the remaining 1 tablespoon of olive oil to the center of the pan. Place the chicken cubes in the center and let them cook for about 6 minutes, stirring often until golden brown.
2. Mix in the tomato paste and tarragon. Add the chicken stock and stir well to combine everything. Bring the mixture to a boil. Add the pappardelle. Simmer covered for 9-11 minutes, stirring occasionally, until the pasta is cooked and the liquid is mostly absorbed. Remove the pan from the heat. Stir 2 tbsp of the hot liquid from the pan into the yogurt. Pour the tempered yogurt into the pan and stir well to mix it into the sauce. Season with salt and pepper. Top with pepper flakes.

Nutrition Info:

• Info Per Serving: Calories: 556;Fat: 18g;Protein: 42g;Carbs: 56g.

Spanish Chicken Skillet

Servings:4
Cooking Time:25 Minutes

Ingredients:

- 2 tbsp olive oil
- ½ cup chicken stock
- 4 chicken breasts
- 2 garlic cloves, minced
- 1 celery stalk, chopped
- 1 tbsp oregano, dried
- Salt and black pepper to taste
- 1 white onion, chopped
- 1 ½ cups tomatoes, cubed
- 10 green olives, sliced

Directions:

1. Warm the olive oil in a skillet over medium heat. Season the chicken with salt and pepper and cook for 4 minutes on both sides. Stir in garlic, oregano, stock, onion, celery, tomatoes, and olives and bring to a boil. Simmer for 13-15 minutes.

Nutrition Info:

- Info Per Serving: Calories: 140;Fat: 7g;Protein: 11g;Carbs: 13g.

Baked Root Veggie & Chicken

Servings:6
Cooking Time:50 Minutes

Ingredients:

- 2 sweet potatoes, peeled and cubed
- ½ cup green olives, pitted and smashed
- ¼ cup olive oil
- 2 lb chicken breasts, sliced
- 2 tbsp harissa seasoning
- 1 lemon, zested and juiced
- Salt and black pepper to taste
- 2 carrots, chopped
- 1 onion, chopped
- ½ cup feta cheese, crumbled
- ½ cup parsley, chopped

Directions:

1. Preheat the oven to 390 F. Place chicken, harissa seasoning, lemon juice, lemon zest, olive oil, salt, pepper, carrots, sweet potatoes, and onion in a roasting pan and mix well. Bake for 40 minutes. Combine feta cheese and green olives in a bowl. Share chicken mixture into plates and top with olive mixture. Top with parsley and parsley and serve immediately.

Nutrition Info:

- Info Per Serving: Calories: 310;Fat: 10g;Protein: 15g;Carbs: 23g.

Beans , Grains, And Pastas Recipes

Mediterranean Brown Rice

Servings:4
Cooking Time:20 Minutes

Ingredients:

- 1 lb asparagus, steamed and chopped
- 2 tbsp olive oil
- 3 tbsp balsamic vinegar
- 1 cup brown rice
- 2 tsp mustard
- Salt and black pepper to taste
- 5 oz baby spinach
- ½ cup parsley, chopped
- 1 tbsp tarragon, chopped

Directions:

1. Bring to a boil a pot of salted water over medium heat. Add in brown rice and cook for 7-9 minutes until al dente. Drain and place in a bowl. Add the asparagus to the same pot and blanch them for 4-5 minutes. Remove them to the rice bowl. Mix in spinach, olive oil, balsamic vinegar, mustard, salt, pepper, parsley, and tarragon. Serve.

Nutrition Info:

- Info Per Serving: Calories: 330;Fat: 12g;Protein: 11g;Carbs: 17g.

Veggie & Beef Ragu

Servings:4
Cooking Time:20 Minutes

Ingredients:

- 2 tbsp butter
- 16 oz tagliatelle pasta
- 1 lb ground beef
- Salt and black pepper to taste
- ¼ cup tomato sauce
- 1 green bell pepper, chopped
- 1 red bell pepper, chopped
- 1 small red onion, chopped
- 1 cup grated Parmesan cheese

Directions:

1. In a pot of boiling water, cook the tagliatelle pasta for 8-10 minutes until al dente. Drain and set aside.
2. Heat half of the butter in a medium skillet and cook the beef until brown, 5 minutes. Season with salt and black pepper. Stir in the tomato sauce and cook for 10 minutes or until the sauce reduces by a quarter. Stir in the bell peppers and onion; cook for 1 minute and turn the heat off. Adjust the taste with salt and black pepper and mix in the tagliatelle. Dish the food onto serving plates. Garnish with Parmesan.

Nutrition Info:

- Info Per Serving: Calories: 451;Fat: 26g;Protein: 39g;Carbs: 6g.

Spanakopita Macaroni With Cheese

Servings:3
Cooking Time:15 Minutes

Ingredients:

- ½ lb leftover macaroni, cooked
- 4 tbsp butter
- 1 garlic clove, minced
- 1 lb spinach, torn
- 1 cup whole milk
- 1/3 cup feta cheese, crumbled
- ¼ tsp ground nutmeg
- 1 tsp dried Greek oregano
- 1 tsp lemon juice

Directions:

1. Melt the butter in a saucepan over medium heat. Stir in garlic and nutmeg for 1 minute. Slowly add the milk and spinach and cook for 3 minutes. Add the feta and oregano. Continue stirring with a whisk until the mixture thickens. Add the pasta and lemon juice and stir until everything is heated through. Serve immediately.

Nutrition Info:

- Info Per Serving: Calories: 499;Fat: 30g;Protein: 19g;Carbs: 42g.

Cranberry And Almond Quinoa

Servings:2
Cooking Time: 10 Minutes

Ingredients:

- 2 cups water
- 1 cup quinoa, rinsed
- ¼ cup salted sunflower seeds
- ½ cup slivered almonds
- 1 cup dried cranberries

Directions:

1. Combine water and quinoa in the Instant Pot.
2. Secure the lid. Select the Manual mode and set the cooking time for 10 minutes at High Pressure.
3. Once cooking is complete, do a quick pressure release. Carefully open the lid.
4. Add sunflower seeds, almonds, and dried cranberries and gently mix until well combined.
5. Serve hot.

Nutrition Info:

- Info Per Serving: Calories: 445;Fat: 14.8g;Protein: 15.1g;Carbs: 64.1g.

Turkish-style Orzo

Servings:2
Cooking Time:10 Minutes

Ingredients:

- 1 cup dry orzo
- 1 cup halved grape tomatoes
- 1 bag baby spinach
- 2 tbsp extra-virgin olive oil
- Salt and black pepper to taste
- ¾ cup feta cheese, crumbled
- 1 lemon, juiced and zested
- 1 tbsp fresh dill, chopped

Directions:

1. In a pot of boiling water, cook the orzo for 8 minutes. Drain well and return to the pot. Add in the tomatoes and spinach and cook until the spinach is wilted, 4-5 minutes. Mix in the olive oil, salt, and pepper. Top the dish with feta, dill, lemon juice, and lemon zest, then toss to coat. Serve and enjoy!

Nutrition Info:

- Info Per Serving: Calories: 612;Fat: 27g;Protein: 22g;Carbs: 74g.

Rigatoni With Peppers & Mozzarella

Servings:4
Cooking Time:30 Min + Marinating Time

Ingredients:

- 1 lb fresh mozzarella cheese, cubed
- 3 tbsp olive oil
- ¼ cup chopped fresh chives
- ¼ cup basil, chopped
- ½ tsp red pepper flakes
- 1 tsp apple cider vinegar
- Salt and black pepper to taste
- 3 garlic cloves, minced
- 2 cups sliced onions
- 3 cups bell peppers, sliced
- 2 cups tomato sauce
- 8 oz rigatoni
- 1 tbsp butter
- ¼ cup grated Parmesan cheese

Directions:

1. Bring to a boil salted water in a pot over high heat. Add the rigatoni and cook according to package directions. Drain and set aside, reserving 1 cup of the cooking water. Combine the mozzarella, 1 tablespoon of olive oil, chives, basil, pepper flakes, apple cider vinegar, salt, and pepper. Let the cheese marinate for 30 minutes at room temperature.
2. Warm the remaining olive oil in a large skillet over medium heat. Stir-fry the garlic for 10 seconds and add the onions and peppers. Cook for 3-4 minutes, stirring occasionally until the onions are translucent. Pour in the tomato sauce, and reduce the heat to a simmer. Add the rigatoni and reserved cooking water and toss to coat. Heat off and adjust the seasoning with salt and pepper. Toss with marinated mozzarella cheese and butter. Sprinkle with Parmesan cheese and serve.

Nutrition Info:

- Info Per Serving: Calories: 434;Fat: 18g;Protein: 44g;Carbs: 27g.

Ritzy Veggie Chili

Servings:4
Cooking Time: 5 Hours

Ingredients:

- 1 can chopped tomatoes, with the juice
- 1 can black beans, drained and rinsed
- 1 can red beans, drained and rinsed
- 1 medium green bell pepper, chopped
- 1 yellow onion, chopped
- 1 tablespoon onion powder
- 1 teaspoon paprika
- 1 teaspoon cayenne pepper
- 1 teaspoon garlic powder
- ½ teaspoon sea salt
- ½ teaspoon ground black pepper
- 1 tablespoon olive oil
- 1 large hass avocado, pitted, peeled, and chopped, for garnish

Directions:

1. Combine all the ingredients, except for the avocado, in the slow cooker. Stir to mix well.
2. Put the slow cooker lid on and cook on high for 5 hours or until the vegetables are tender and the mixture has a thick consistency.
3. Pour the chili in a large serving bowl. Allow to cool for 30 minutes, then spread with chopped avocado and serve.

Nutrition Info:

- Info Per Serving: Calories: 633;Fat: 16.3g;Protein: 31.7g;Carbs: 97.0g.

Hearty Butternut Spinach, And Cheeses Lasagna

Servings:4
Cooking Time: 3 Hours 45 Minutes

Ingredients:

- 2 tablespoons extra-virgin olive oil, divided
- 1 butternut squash, halved lengthwise and deseeded
- ½ teaspoon sage
- ½ teaspoon sea salt
- ¼ teaspoon ground black pepper
- ¼ cup grated Parmesan cheese
- 2 cups ricotta cheese
- ½ cup unsweetened almond milk
- 5 layers whole-wheat lasagna noodles
- 4 ounces fresh spinach leaves, divided
- ½ cup shredded part skim Mozzarella, for garnish

Directions:

1. Preheat the oven to 400ºF. Line a baking sheet with parchment paper.
2. Brush 1 tablespoon of olive oil on the cut side of the butternut squash, then place the squash on the baking sheet.
3. Bake in the preheated oven for 45 minutes or until the squash is tender.
4. Allow to cool until you can handle it, then scoop the flesh out and put the flesh in a food processor to purée.
5. Combine the puréed butternut squash flesh with sage, salt, and ground black pepper in a large bowl. Stir to mix well.
6. Combine the cheeses and milk in a separate bowl, then sprinkle with salt and pepper, to taste.
7. Grease the slow cooker with 1 tablespoon of olive oil, then add a layer of lasagna noodles to coat the bottom of the slow cooker.
8. Spread half of the squash mixture on top of the noodles, then top the squash mixture with another layer of lasagna noodles.
9. Spread half of the spinach over the noodles, then top the spinach with half of cheese mixture. Repeat with remaining 3 layers of lasagna noodles, squash mixture, spinach, and cheese mixture.
10. Top the cheese mixture with Mozzarella, then put the lid on and cook on low for 3 hours or until the lasagna noodles are al dente.
11. Serve immediately.

Nutrition Info:

- Info Per Serving: Calories: 657;Fat: 37.1g;Protein: 30.9g;Carbs: 57.2g.

Traditional Beef Lasagna

Servings:4
Cooking Time:70 Minutes

Ingredients:

- 2 tbsp olive oil
- 1 lb lasagne sheets
- 1 lb ground beef
- 1 white onion, chopped
- 1 tsp Italian seasoning
- Salt and black pepper to taste
- 1 cup marinara sauce
- ½ cup grated Parmesan cheese

Directions:

1. Preheat oven to 350 F. Warm olive oil in a skillet and add the beef and onion. Cook until the beef is brown, 7-8 minutes. Season with Italian seasoning, salt, and pepper. Cook for 1 minute and mix in the marinara sauce. Simmer for 3 minutes.
2. Spread a layer of the beef mixture in a lightly greased baking sheet and make a first single layer on the beef mixture. Top with a single layer of lasagna sheets. Repeat the layering two more times using the remaining ingredients in the same quantities. Sprinkle with Parmesan cheese. Bake in the oven until the cheese melts and is bubbly with the sauce, 20 minutes. Remove the lasagna, allow cooling for 2 minutes and dish onto serving plates. Serve warm.

Nutrition Info:

- Info Per Serving: Calories: 557;Fat: 29g;Protein: 60g;Carbs: 4g.

Baked Rolled Oat With Pears And Pecans

Servings:6
Cooking Time: 30 Minutes

Ingredients:

- 2 tablespoons coconut oil, melted, plus more for greasing the pan
- 3 ripe pears, cored and diced
- 2 cups unsweetened almond milk
- 1 tablespoon pure vanilla extract
- ¼ cup pure maple syrup
- 2 cups gluten-free rolled oats
- ½ cup raisins
- ¾ cup chopped pecans
- ¼ teaspoon ground nutmeg
- 1 teaspoon ground cinnamon
- ½ teaspoon ground ginger
- ¼ teaspoon sea salt

Directions:

1. Preheat the oven to 350°F. Grease a baking dish with melted coconut oil, then spread the pears in a single layer on the baking dish evenly.
2. Combine the almond milk, vanilla extract, maple syrup, and coconut oil in a bowl. Stir to mix well.
3. Combine the remaining ingredients in a separate large bowl. Stir to mix well. Fold the almond milk mixture in the bowl, then pour the mixture over the pears.
4. Place the baking dish in the preheated oven and bake for 30 minutes or until lightly browned and set.
5. Serve immediately.

Nutrition Info:

- Info Per Serving: Calories: 479;Fat: 34.9g;Protein: 8.8g;Carbs: 50.1g.

Leftover Pasta & Mushroom Frittata

Servings:4
Cooking Time:25 Minutes

Ingredients:

- 2 tbsp olive oil
- 4 oz leftover spaghetti, cooked
- 8 large eggs, beaten
- ¼ cup heavy cream
- ½ tsp Italian seasoning
- ½ tsp garlic salt
- 1/8 tsp garlic pepper
- 1 cup chopped mushrooms
- 1 cup Pecorino cheese, grated

Directions:

1. Preheat your broiler. Warm the olive oil in a large skillet over medium heat. Add mushrooms and cook for 3–4 minutes, until almost tender. In a large bowl, beat the eggs with cream, Italian seasoning, garlic salt, and garlic pepper. Stir in the leftover spaghetti. Pour the egg mixture over the mushrooms and level with a spatula. Cook for 5–7 minutes until the eggs are almost set. Sprinkle with cheese and place under broiler for 3–5 minutes, until the cheese melts. Serve.

Nutrition Info:

- Info Per Serving: Calories: 400;Fat: 30g;Protein: 23g;Carbs: 11g.

Autumn Vegetable & Rigatoni Bake

Servings:6
Cooking Time:45 Minutes

Ingredients:

- 2 tbsp grated Pecorino-Romano cheese
- 2 tbsp olive oil
- 1 lb pumpkin, chopped
- 1 zucchini, chopped
- 1 onion, chopped
- 1 lb rigatoni
- Salt and black pepper to taste
- ½ tsp garlic powder

- ½ cup dry white wine

Directions:

1. Preheat oven to 420 F. Combine zucchini, pumpkin, onion, and olive oil in a bowl. Arrange on a lined aluminum foil sheet and season with salt, pepper, and garlic powder. Bake for 30 minutes until tender. In a pot of boiling water, cook rigatoni for 8-10 minutes until al dente. Drain and set aside.
2. In a food processor, place ½ cup of the roasted veggies and wine and pulse until smooth. Transfer to a skillet over medium heat. Stir in rigatoni and cook until heated through. Top with the remaining vegetables and Pecorino cheese to serve.

Nutrition Info:

- Info Per Serving: Calories: 186;Fat: 11g;Protein: 10g;Carbs: 15g.

Pea & Mint Tortellini

Servings:4
Cooking Time:30 Minutes

Ingredients:

- 1 package frozen cheese tortellini
- 2 tbsp olive oil
- 3 garlic cloves, minced
- ½ cup vegetable broth
- 2 cups frozen baby peas
- 1 lemon, zested
- 2 tbsp mint leaves, chopped

Directions:

1. Bring to a boil salted water in a pot over high heat. Add the tortellini and cook according to package directions. Drain and transfer to a bowl. Warm the olive oil in a large saucepan over medium and sauté the garlic for 2 minutes until golden. Pour in the broth and peas and bring to a simmer. Add in the tortellini and cook for 4–5 minutes until the mixture is slightly thickened. Stir in lemon zest, top with mint, and serve.

Nutrition Info:

- Info Per Serving: Calories: 272;Fat: 11g;Protein: 11g;Carbs: 34g.

Paprika Spinach & Chickpea Bowl

Servings:4
Cooking Time:20 Minutes

Ingredients:

- 2 tbsp olive oil
- 1 lb canned chickpeas
- 10 oz spinach
- 1 tsp coriander seeds
- 1 red onion, finely chopped
- 2 tomatoes, pureed
- 1 garlic clove, minced
- ½ tbsp rosemary
- ½ tsp smoked paprika
- Salt and white pepper to taste

Directions:

1. Heat the olive oil in a pot over medium heat. Add in the onion, garlic, coriander seeds, salt, and pepper and cook for 3 minutes until translucent. Stir in tomatoes, rosemary, paprika, salt, and white pepper. Bring to a boil, then lower the heat, and simmer for 10 minutes. Add in chickpeas and spinach and cook covered until the spinach wilts. Serve.

Nutrition Info:

- Info Per Serving: Calories: 512;Fat: 1.8g;Protein: 25g;Carbs: 76g.

Bean & Egg Noodles With Lemon Sauce

Servings:4
Cooking Time:20 Minutes

Ingredients:

- 3 tbsp olive oil
- 12 oz egg noodles
- 1 can diced tomatoes
- 1 can cannellini beans
- ½ cup heavy cream
- 1 cup vegetable stock
- 2 garlic cloves, minced
- 1 onion, chopped
- 1 cup spinach, chopped
- 1 tsp dill
- 1 tsp thyme
- ½ tsp red pepper, crushed
- 1 tsp lemon juice
- 1 tbsp fresh basil, chopped

Directions:

1. Warm the olive oil in a pot over medium heat. Add in onion and garlic and cook for 3 minutes until softened. Stir in dill, thyme, and red pepper for 1 minute. Add in spinach, vegetable stock, and tomatoes. Bring to a boil, add the egg noodles, cover, and lower the heat. Cook for 5-7 minutes. Put in beans and cook until heated through. Combine the heavy cream, lemon juice, and basil. Serve the dish with creamy lemon sauce on the side.

Nutrition Info:

- Info Per Serving: Calories: 641;Fat: 19g;Protein: 28g;Carbs: 92g.

Easy Simple Pesto Pasta

Servings:4
Cooking Time: 8 Minutes

Ingredients:

- 1 pound spaghetti
- 4 cups fresh basil leaves, stems removed
- 3 cloves garlic
- 1 teaspoon salt
- ½ teaspoon freshly ground black pepper
- ½ cup toasted pine nuts
- ¼ cup lemon juice
- ½ cup grated Parmesan cheese
- 1 cup extra-virgin olive oil

Directions:

1. Bring a large pot of salted water to a boil. Add the spaghetti to the pot and cook for 8 minutes.
2. In a food processor, place the remaining ingredients, except for the olive oil, and pulse.
3. While the processor is running, slowly drizzle the olive oil through the top opening. Process until all the olive oil has been added.
4. Reserve ½ cup of the cooking liquid. Drain the pasta and put it into a large bowl. Add the pesto and cooking liquid to the bowl of pasta and toss everything together.
5. Serve immediately.

Nutrition Info:

- Info Per Serving: Calories: 1067;Fat: 72.0g;Protein: 23.0g;Carbs: 91g.

Minestrone Chickpeas And Macaroni Casserole

Servings:5
Cooking Time: 7 Hours 20 Minutes

Ingredients:

- 1 can chickpeas, drained and rinsed
- 1 can diced tomatoes, with the juice
- 1 can no-salt-added tomato paste
- 3 medium carrots, sliced
- 3 cloves garlic, minced
- 1 medium yellow onion, chopped
- 1 cup low-sodium vegetable soup
- ½ teaspoon dried rosemary
- 1 teaspoon dried oregano
- 2 teaspoons maple syrup
- ½ teaspoon sea salt
- ¼ teaspoon ground black pepper
- ½ pound fresh green beans, trimmed and cut into bite-size pieces
- 1 cup macaroni pasta
- 2 ounces Parmesan cheese, grated

Directions:

1. Except for the green beans, pasta, and Parmesan cheese, combine all the ingredients in the slow cooker and stir to mix well.
2. Put the slow cooker lid on and cook on low for 7 hours.
3. Fold in the pasta and green beans. Put the lid on and cook on high for 20 minutes or until the vegetable are soft and the pasta is al dente.
4. Pour them in a large serving bowl and spread with Parmesan cheese before serving.

Nutrition Info:

- Info Per Serving: Calories: 349;Fat: 6.7g;Protein: 16.5g;Carbs: 59.9g.

Cranberry & Walnut Freekeh Pilaf

Servings:4
Cooking Time:30 Minutes

Ingredients:

- 2 tbsp olive oil
- 2 ½ cups freekeh, soaked
- 2 medium onions, diced
- ¼ tsp ground cinnamon
- ¼ tsp ground allspice
- ¼ tsp ground nutmeg

- 5 cups chicken stock
- ½ cup walnuts, chopped
- Salt and black pepper to taste
- ½ cup Greek yogurt
- 1 ½ tsp lemon juice
- ½ tsp garlic powder
- 1 tbsp dried cranberries

Directions:

1. Warm the olive oil in a large skillet over medium heat and sauté the onions and cook until fragrant. Add the freekeh, cinnamon, nutmeg, and allspice. Stir for 1 minute. Pour in the stock, cranberries, and walnuts and season with salt and pepper. Bring to a simmer. Cover and reduce the heat to low.
2. Simmer for 15 minutes until the freekeh is tender. Remove from the heat and leave to sit for 5 minutes. In a small bowl, mix the yogurt, lemon juice, and garlic powder. Add the yogurt mixture to the freekeh and serve immediately.

Nutrition Info:

- Info Per Serving: Calories: 650;Fat: 25g;Protein: 12g;Carbs: 91g.

Veggie & Egg Quinoa With Pancetta

Servings:4
Cooking Time:35 Minutes

Ingredients:

- 4 pancetta slices, cooked and crumbled
- 2 tbsp olive oil
- 1 small red onion, chopped
- 1 red bell pepper, chopped
- 1 sweet potato, grated
- 1 green bell pepper, chopped
- 2 garlic cloves, minced
- 1 cup mushrooms, sliced
- ½ cup quinoa
- 1 cup chicken stock
- 4 eggs, fried
- ¼ tsp red pepper flakes
- Salt and black pepper to taste

Directions:

1. Warm the olive oil in a skillet over medium heat and cook onion, garlic, bell peppers, sweet potato, and mushrooms for 5 minutes, stirring often. Stir in quinoa for another minute. Mix in stock, salt, and pepper for 15 minutes. Share into plates and serve topped with fried eggs, salt, pepper, red pepper flakes, and crumbled pancetta.

Nutrition Info:

- Info Per Serving: Calories: 310;Fat: 15g;Protein: 16g;Carbs: 26g.

Carrot & Barley Risotto

Servings:6
Cooking Time:1 Hour 20 Minutes

Ingredients:

- 2 tbsp olive oil
- 4 cups vegetable broth
- 4 cups water
- 1 onion, chopped fine
- 1 carrot, chopped
- 1 ½ cups pearl barley
- 1 cup dry white wine
- ¼ tsp dried oregano
- 2 oz Parmesan cheese, grated
- Salt and black pepper to taste

Directions:

1. Bring broth and water to a simmer in a saucepan. Reduce heat to low and cover to keep warm.
2. Heat 1 tbsp of oil in a pot over medium heat until sizzling. Stir-fry onion and carrot until softened, 6-7 minutes. Add barley and cook, stirring often, until lightly toasted and aromatic, 4 minutes. Add wine and cook, stirring frequently for 2 minutes. Stir in 3 cups of water and oregano, bring to a simmer, and cook, stirring occasionally until liquid is absorbed, 25 minutes. Stir in 2 cups of broth, bring to a simmer, and cook until the liquid is absorbed, 15 minutes.
3. Continue cooking, stirring often and adding warm broth as needed to prevent the pot bottom from becoming dry until barley is cooked through but still somewhat firm in the center, 15-20 minutes. Off heat, adjust consistency with the remaining warm broth as needed. Stir in Parmesan and the remaining oil and season with salt and pepper to taste. Serve.

Nutrition Info:

- Info Per Serving: Calories: 355;Fat: 21g;Protein: 16g;Carbs: 35g.

Kale Chicken With Pappardelle

Servings:4

Cooking Time:30 Min + Chilling Time

Ingredients:

- 1 cup grated Parmigiano-Reggiano cheese
- 4 chicken thighs, cut into 1-inch pieces
- 3 tbsp olive oil
- 16 oz pappardelle pasta
- Salt and black pepper to taste
- 1 yellow onion, chopped
- 4 garlic cloves, minced
- 12 cherry tomatoes, halved
- ½ cup chicken broth
- 2 cups baby kale, chopped
- 2 tbsp pine nuts for topping

Directions:

1. In a pot of boiling water, cook the pappardelle pasta for 8-10 minutes until al dente. Drain and set aside.
2. Heat the olive oil in a medium pot. Season the chicken with salt and pepper and sear in the oil until golden brown on the outside. Transfer to a plate and set aside. Add the onion and garlic to the oil and cook until softened and fragrant, 3 minutes. Mix in tomatoes and chicken broth and cook over low heat until the tomatoes soften and the liquid reduces by half. Season with salt and pepper. Return the chicken to the pot and stir in kale. Allow wilting for 2 minutes. Spoon the pappardelle onto serving plates, top with kale sauce and Parmigianino-Reggiano cheese. Garnish with pine nuts.

Nutrition Info:

- Info Per Serving: Calories: 740;Fat: 53g;Protein: 50g;Carbs: 15g.

Quinoa With Baby Potatoes And Broccoli

Servings:4

Cooking Time: 10 Minutes

Ingredients:

- 2 tablespoons olive oil
- 1 cup baby potatoes, cut in half
- 1 cup broccoli florets
- 2 cups cooked quinoa
- Zest of 1 lemon
- Sea salt and freshly ground pepper, to taste

Directions:

1. Heat the olive oil in a large skillet over medium heat until shimmering.
2. Add the potatoes and cook for about 6 to 7 minutes, or until softened and golden brown. Add the broccoli and cook for about 3 minutes, or until tender.
3. Remove from the heat and add the quinoa and lemon zest. Season with salt and pepper to taste, then serve.

Nutrition Info:

- Info Per Serving: Calories: 205;Fat: 8.6g;Protein: 5.1g;Carbs: 27.3g.

Friday Night Penne In Tomato Sauce

Servings:6

Cooking Time:60 Minutes

Ingredients:

- ¼ cup olive oil
- 1 shallot, sliced thin
- 2 lb cherry tomatoes, halved
- 3 garlic cloves, sliced thin
- 1 tbsp balsamic vinegar
- 1 tbsp sugar
- Salt and black pepper to taste
- ¼ tsp red pepper flakes
- 1 lb penne
- ¼ cup oregano, chopped
- Grated Pecorino cheese

Directions:

1. Preheat oven to 350F. In a bowl, drizzle shallot with some olive oil and mix well. In a separate bowl, gently add the tomatoes, remaining oil, garlic, vinegar, sugar, red pepper flakes, salt, and pepper. Spread tomato mixture in even layer in a rimmed baking sheet, spread shallot over the tomatoes, and roast until edges of the shallot begin to brown and tomato skins are slightly shriveled, 33-38 minutes; do not stir. Let cool for 5 to 10 minutes.
2. Meanwhile, fill a large pot with water and bring to a boil. Add the pasta and a pinch of salt and cook until al dente. Reserve ½ cup of cooking liquid, drain pasta and return it to the pot. Using a spatula, scrape tomato mixture onto the pasta. Add oregano and toss to combine. Season to taste and adjust consistency with the cooking water. Serve topped with Pecorino cheese.

Nutrition Info:

- Info Per Serving: Calories: 423;Fat: 16g;Protein:

15g;Carbs: 45g.

Spanish-style Linguine With Tapenade

Servings:4
Cooking Time:20 Minutes

Ingredients:

- 1 cup black olives, pitted
- 2 tbsp capers
- 2 tbsp rosemary, chopped
- 1 garlic clove, smashed
- 2 anchovy fillets, chopped
- ½ tsp sugar
- ⅔ cup + 2 tbsp olive oil
- 1 lb linguine
- ½ cup grated Manchego cheese
- 1 tbsp chopped fresh chives

Directions:

1. Process the olives, capers, rosemary, garlic, anchovies, sugar, and ⅔ cup olive oil in your food processor until well incorporated but not smooth; set aside. Bring a large pot of salted water to a boil, add the linguine, and cook for 7-9 minutes until al dente. Drain the pasta in a bowl and add the remaining 2 tablespoons olive oil and Manchego cheese; toss to coat. Arrange pasta on a serving platter and top it with tapenade and chives. Serve and enjoy!

Nutrition Info:

- Info Per Serving: Calories: 375;Fat: 39g;Protein: 5g;Carbs: 23g.

Old-fashioned Pasta Primavera

Servings:4
Cooking Time:25 Minutes

Ingredients:

- ½ cup grated Pecorino Romano cheese
- 2 cups cauliflower florets, cut into matchsticks
- ¼ cup olive oil
- 16 oz tortiglioni
- ½ cup chopped green onions
- 1 red bell pepper, sliced
- 4 garlic cloves, minced
- 1 cup grape tomatoes, halved
- 2 tsp dried Italian seasoning
- ½ lemon, juiced

Directions:

1. In a pot of boiling water, cook the tortiglioni pasta for 8-10 minutes until al dente. Drain and set aside.
2. Heat olive oil in a skillet and sauté onion, cauliflower, and bell pepper for 7 minutes. Mix in garlic and cook until fragrant, 30 seconds. Stir in the tomatoes and Italian seasoning; cook until the tomatoes soften, 5 minutes. Mix in the lemon juice and tortiglioni. Garnish with cheese.

Nutrition Info:

- Info Per Serving: Calories: 283;Fat: 18g;Protein: 15g;Carbs: 5g.

Tortellini & Cannellini With Meatballs

Servings:4
Cooking Time:30 Minutes

Ingredients:

- 2 tbsp parsley, chopped
- 12 oz fresh tortellini
- 3 tbsp olive oil
- 5 cloves garlic, minced
- ½ lb meatballs
- 1 can cannellini beans
- 1 can roasted tomatoes
- Salt and black pepper to taste

Directions:

1. Bring to a boil salted water in a pot over high heat. Add the tortellini and cook according to package directions. Drain and set aside. Warm the olive oil in a large skillet over medium heat and sauté the garlic for 1 minute. Stir in meatballs and brown for 4–5 minutes on all sides. Add the tomatoes and cannellini and continue to cook for 5 minutes or until heated through. Adjust the seasoning with salt and pepper. Stir in tortellini. Sprinkle with parsley and serve.

Nutrition Info:

- Info Per Serving: Calories: 578;Fat: 30g;Protein: 25g;Carbs: 58g.

Black Bean & Chickpea Burgers

Servings:4
Cooking Time:35 Minutes

Ingredients:

- 1 tsp olive oil
- 1 can black beans
- 1 can chickpeas
- ½ white onion, chopped
- 2 garlic cloves, minced
- 2 free-range eggs
- 1 tsp ground cumin
- Salt and black pepper to taste
- 1 cup panko breadcrumbs
- ½ cup old-fashioned rolled oats
- 6 hamburger buns, halved
- 2 avocados
- 2 tbsp lemon juice
- 6 large lettuce leaves

Directions:

1. Preheat oven to 380 F. Blitz the black beans, chickpeas, eggs, cumin, salt, and pepper in a food processor until smooth. Transfer the mixture to a bowl and add the onion and garlic and mix well. Stir in the bread crumbs and oats. Shape the mixture into 6 balls, flatten them with your hands to make patties. Brush both sides of the burgers with oil. Arrange them on a parchment-lined baking sheet. Bake for 30 minutes, flippingonce until slightly crispy on the edges.
2. Meanwhile, mash the avocado with the lemon juice and a pinch of salt with a fork until smooth; set aside. Toast the buns for 2-3 minutes. Spread the avocado mixture onto the base of each bun, then top with the burgers and lettuce leaves. Finish with the bun tops. Serve and enjoy!

Nutrition Info:

- Info Per Serving: Calories: 867;Fat: 22g;Protein: 39g;Carbs: 133g.

Spicy Bean Rolls

Servings:4
Cooking Time:25 Minutes

Ingredients:

- 1 tbsp olive oil
- 1 red onion, chopped
- 2 garlic cloves, minced
- 1 green bell pepper, sliced
- 2 cups canned cannellini beans
- 1 red chili pepper, chopped
- 1 tbsp cilantro, chopped
- 1 tsp cumin, ground
- Salt and black pepper to taste
- 4 whole-wheat tortillas
- 1 cup mozzarella, shredded

Directions:

1. Warm the olive oil in a skillet over medium heat and sauté onion for 3 minutes. Stir in garlic, bell pepper, cannellini beans, red chili pepper, cilantro, cumin, salt, and pepper and cook for 15 minutes. Spoon bean mixture on each tortilla and top with cheese. Roll up and serve right away.

Nutrition Info:

- Info Per Serving: Calories: 680;Fat: 15g;Protein: 38g;Carbs: 75g.

Brown Rice Pilaf With Pistachios And Raisins

Servings:6
Cooking Time: 15 Minutes

Ingredients:

- 1 tablespoon extra-virgin olive oil
- 1 cup chopped onion
- ½ cup shredded carrot
- ½ teaspoon ground cinnamon
- 1 teaspoon ground cumin
- 2 cups brown rice
- 1¾ cups pure orange juice
- ¼ cup water
- ½ cup shelled pistachios
- 1 cup golden raisins
- ½ cup chopped fresh chives

Directions:

1. Heat the olive oil in a saucepan over medium-high heat until shimmering.
2. Add the onion and sauté for 5 minutes or until translucent.
3. Add the carrots, cinnamon, and cumin, then sauté for 1 minutes or until aromatic.
4. Pour int the brown rice, orange juice, and water. Bring to a boil. Reduce the heat to medium-low and simmer for 7 minutes or until the liquid is almost absorbed.
5. Transfer the rice mixture in a large serving bowl, then spread with pistachios, raisins, and chives. Serve immediately.

Nutrition Info:

- Info Per Serving: Calories: 264;Fat: 7.1g;Protein: 5.2g;Carbs: 48.9g.

Turkish Canned Pinto Bean Salad

Servings:4
Cooking Time: 3 Minutes

Ingredients:

- ¼ cup extra-virgin olive oil, divided
- 3 garlic cloves, lightly crushed and peeled
- 2 cans pinto beans, rinsed
- 2 cups plus 1 tablespoon water
- Salt and pepper, to taste
- ¼ cup tahini
- 3 tablespoons lemon juice
- 1 tablespoon ground dried Aleppo pepper, plus extra for serving
- 8 ounces cherry tomatoes, halved
- ¼ red onion, sliced thinly
- ½ cup fresh parsley leaves
- 2 hard-cooked large eggs, quartered
- 1 tablespoon toasted sesame seeds

Directions:

1. Add 1 tablespoon of the olive oil and garlic to a medium saucepan over medium heat. Cook for about 3 minutes, stirring constantly, or until the garlic turns golden but not brown.
2. Add the beans, 2 cups of the water and 1 teaspoon salt and bring to a simmer. Remove from the heat, cover and let sit for 20 minutes. Drain the beans and discard the garlic.
3. In a large bowl, whisk together the remaining 3 tablespoons of the oil, tahini, lemon juice, Aleppo, the remaining 1 tablespoon of the water and ¼ teaspoon salt. Stir in the beans, tomatoes, onion and parsley. Season with salt and pepper to taste.
4. Transfer to a serving platter and top with the eggs. Sprinkle with the sesame seeds and extra Aleppo before serving.

Nutrition Info:

- Info Per Serving: Calories: 402;Fat: 18.9g;Protein: 16.2g;Carbs: 44.4g.

Fruits, Desserts And Snacks Recipes

Pecan And Carrot Cake

Servings:12
Cooking Time: 45 Minutes

Ingredients:

- ½ cup coconut oil, at room temperature, plus more for greasing the baking dish
- 2 teaspoons pure vanilla extract
- ¼ cup pure maple syrup
- 6 eggs
- ½ cup coconut flour
- 1 teaspoon baking powder
- 1 teaspoon baking soda
- ½ teaspoon ground nutmeg
- 1 teaspoon ground cinnamon
- ⅛ teaspoon sea salt
- ½ cup chopped pecans
- 3 cups finely grated carrots

Directions:

1. Preheat the oven to 350ºF. Grease a 13-by-9-inch baking dish with coconut oil.
2. Combine the vanilla extract, maple syrup, and ½ cup of coconut oil in a large bowl. Stir to mix well.
3. Break the eggs in the bowl and whisk to combine well. Set aside.
4. Combine the coconut flour, baking powder, baking soda, nutmeg, cinnamon, and salt in a separate bowl. Stir to mix well.
5. Make a well in the center of the flour mixture, then pour the egg mixture into the well. Stir to combine well.
6. Add the pecans and carrots to the bowl and toss to mix well. Pour the mixture in the single layer on the baking dish.
7. Bake in the preheated oven for 45 minutes or until puffed and the cake spring back when lightly press with your fingers.
8. Remove the cake from the oven. Allow to cool for at least 15 minutes, then serve.

Nutrition Info:

- Info Per Serving: Calories: 255;Fat: 21.2g;Protein: 5.1g;Carbs: 12.8g.

Mini Meatball Pizza

Servings:4
Cooking Time:25 Minutes

Ingredients:

- 1 pizza crust
- 1 ½ cups pizza sauce
- ½ tsp dried oregano
- 8 oz bite-sized meatballs
- 1 cup bell peppers, sliced
- 2 cups mozzarella, shredded

Directions:

1. Preheat oven to 400 F. Spread the pizza crust evenly with pizza sauce and sprinkle with oregano. Arrange the meatballs on the pizza sauce. Sprinkle with bell peppers and mozzarella cheese. Bake for about 20 minutes or until the crust is golden brown and cheese melts. Serve immediately.

Nutrition Info:

- Info Per Serving: Calories: 555;Fat: 28g;Protein: 30g;Carbs: 45g.

Turkish Dolma (stuffed Grape Leaves)

Servings:4
Cooking Time:50 Minutes

Ingredients:

- 2 tbsp olive oil
- 1 onion, chopped
- 2 garlic cloves, minced
- 1 cup short-grain rice
- ¼ cup gold raisins
- ¼ cup pine nuts, toasted
- 1 lemon, juiced
- ¼ tsp ground cinnamon
- Salt and black pepper to taste
- 2 tbsp parsley, chopped
- 20 preserved grape leaves

Directions:

1. Warm the olive oil in a skillet over medium heat. Add the onion and garlic and sauté for 5 minutes. Add the rice, golden raisins, pine nuts, cinnamon, and lemon juice. Season with salt and pepper. Stuff each leaf with about 1 tablespoon of the filling. Roll tightly and place each in a pot, seam side down. Add 2 cups of water and simmer for about 15-18 minutes. Serve warm.

Nutrition Info:

- Info Per Serving: Calories: 237;Fat: 12g;Protein: 7g;Carbs: 26g.

Cointreau Poached Pears

Servings:4
Cooking Time:60 Minutes

Ingredients:

- 4 Bosc pears, peeled
- ¼ tsp cardamom seeds
- 1 cup orange juice
- 1 cinnamon stick
- 1-star anise
- 1 tbsp Cointreau liqueur
- 1 tsp allspice berries
- 1 tsp orange zest
- 3 cups red wine
- 1 cup sugar
- 1 cup whipping cream

Directions:

1. Place orange liqueur and red wine in a pot over medium heat and bring to a boil. Reduce the heat to low and add the cardamom seeds, cinnamon stick, allspice berries, orange juice, orange zest, and star anise; simmer for 5 minutes. Add in the pears and sugar, cover, and poach for about 25-30 minutes until tender.
2. Remove the pears from the pot and set aside. Drain the cooking liquid through a sieve, then return it to the pot. Bring to a boil and cook until the liquid obtains a syrup-like consistency, about 10-15 minutes. Pour the sauce over the pears, top with whipping cream, and serve.

Nutrition Info:

- Info Per Serving: Calories: 226;Fat: 4.6g;Protein: 11.3g;Carbs: 7g.

Spanish Cheese Crackers

Servings:6
Cooking Time:20 Min + Chilling Time

Ingredients:

- 4 tbsp butter, softened
- 1 cup Manchego cheese, grated
- 1 cup flour
- ¼ tsp dried tarragon
- Salt and black pepper to taste
- 1 large egg

Directions:

1. With an electric mixer, cream together the butter and shredded cheese until well combined and smooth. In a small bowl, combine the flour, salt, and pepper. Gradually add the flour mixture to the cheese, mixing constantly until the dough forms a ball. Wrap tightly with plastic wrap and refrigerate for at least 1 hour.
2. Preheat oven to 350 F. In a small bowl, whisk together the egg with salt. Slice the refrigerated dough into small rounds, about ¼ inch thick, and place on two parchment-lined baking sheets. Brush the tops of the crackers with egg wash and bake until the crackers are golden and crispy, 12-15 minutes. Remove from the oven and allow to cool on a wire rack. Serve cooled.

Nutrition Info:

- Info Per Serving: Calories: 243;Fat: 23g;Protein: 8g;Carbs: 2g.

Spicy Hummus

Servings:6
Cooking Time:10 Minutes

Ingredients:

- 2 tbsp olive oil
- ½ tsp hot paprika
- 1 tsp hot pepper sauce
- 1 tsp ground cumin
- 3 garlic cloves, minced
- 1 can chickpeas
- 2 tbsp tahini
- 2 tbsp chopped fresh parsley
- 1 lemon, juiced and zested
- Salt to taste

Directions:

1. In a food processor, blend chickpeas, tahini, oil,

garlic, lemon juice, lemon zest, salt, cumin, and hot pepper sauce for a minute until smooth. Decorate with parsley and paprika.

Nutrition Info:

- Info Per Serving: Calories: 236;Fat: 8.6g;Protein: 10g;Carbs: 31g.

Italian Popcorn

Servings:6
Cooking Time:20 Minutes

Ingredients:

- 2 tbsp butter, melted
- 1 tbsp truffle oil
- 8 cups air-popped popcorn
- 2 tbsp packed brown sugar
- 2 tbsp Italian seasoning
- ¼ tsp sea salt

Directions:

1. Preheat oven to 350 F. Combine butter, Italian seasoning, sugar, and salt in a bowl. Pour over the popcorn and toss well to coat. Remove to a baking dish and bake for 15 minutes, stirring frequently. Drizzle with truffle oil and serve.

Nutrition Info:

- Info Per Serving: Calories: 80;Fat: 5g;Protein: 1.1g;-Carbs: 8.4g.

Speedy Cucumber Canapes

Servings:4
Cooking Time:5 Minutes

Ingredients:

- 2 tbsp olive oil
- 2 cucumbers, sliced into rounds
- 12 cherry tomatoes, halved
- Salt and black pepper to taste
- 1 red chili pepper, dried
- 8 oz cream cheese, softened
- 1 tbsp balsamic vinegar
- 1 tsp chives, chopped

Directions:

1. In a bowl, mix cream cheese, balsamic vinegar, olive oil, chili pepper, and chives. Season with salt and pepper. Spread the mixture over the cucumber rounds and top with the cherry tomato halves. Serve.

Nutrition Info:

- Info Per Serving: Calories: 130;Fat: 3g;Protein: 3g;-Carbs: 7g.

Lovely Coconut-covered Strawberries

Servings:4
Cooking Time:15 Min + Cooling Time

Ingredients:

- 1 cup chocolate chips
- ¼ cup coconut flakes
- 1 lb strawberries
- ½ tsp vanilla extract
- ½ tsp ground nutmeg
- ¼ tsp salt

Directions:

1. Melt chocolate chips for 30 seconds. Remove and stir in vanilla, nutmeg, and salt. Let cool for 2-3 minutes. Dip strawberries into the chocolate and then into the coconut flakes. Place on a wax paper-lined cookie sheet and let sit for 30 minutes until the chocolate dries. Serve.

Nutrition Info:

- Info Per Serving: Calories: 275;Fat: 20g;Protein: 6g;Carbs: 21g.

Sicilian Sandwich Muffuletta

Servings:6
Cooking Time:10 Minutes

Ingredients:

- 1 focaccia bread
- 2 tbsp drained capers
- 2 tbsp black olive tapenade
- ½ lb fontina cheese, sliced
- ¼ lb smoked turkey, sliced
- ¼ lb salami, thinly sliced

Directions:

1. Slice the focaccia bread in half horizontally. Spread each piece with olive tapenade. Layer half of the fontina cheese, a layer of capers, smoked turkey, olive tapenade, salami, capers, and finish with fontina cheese. Top with the remaining focaccia half and press the sandwich together gently. Serve sliced into wedges.

Nutrition Info:

- Info Per Serving: Calories: 335;Fat: 27g;Protein: 18g;Carbs: 4g.

Artichoke & Sun-dried Tomato Pizza

Servings:4
Cooking Time:80 Minutes

Ingredients:

- 2 tbsp olive oil
- 1 cup canned passata
- 2 cups flour
- 1 pinch of sugar
- 1 tsp active dry yeast
- ¾ tsp salt
- 1 ½ cups artichoke hearts
- ¼ cup grated Asiago cheese
- ½ onion, minced
- 3 garlic cloves, minced
- 1 tbsp dried oregano
- 6 sundried tomatoes, chopped
- ½ tsp red pepper flakes
- 5-6 basil leaves, torn

Directions:

1. Sift the flour and salt in a bowl and stir in yeast. Mix 1 cup of lukewarm water, olive oil, and sugar in another bowl. Add the wet mixture to the dry mixture and whisk until you obtain a soft dough. Place the dough on a lightly floured work surface and knead it thoroughly for 4-5 minutes until elastic. Transfer the dough to a greased bowl. Cover with cling film and leave to rise for 50-60 minutes in a warm place until doubled in size. Roll out the dough to a thickness of around 12 inches.
2. Preheat oven to 400 F. Warm oil in a saucepan over medium heat and sauté onion and garlic for 3-4 minutes. Mix in tomatoes and oregano and bring to a boil. Decrease the heat and simmer for another 5 minutes. Transfer the pizza crust to a baking sheet. Spread the sauce all over and top with artichoke hearts and sun-dried tomatoes. Scatter the cheese and bake for 15 minutes until golden. Top with red pepper flakes and basil leaves and serve sliced.

Nutrition Info:

- Info Per Serving: Calories: 254;Fat: 9.5g;Protein: 8g;Carbs: 34.3g.

Pomegranate Blueberry Granita

Servings:2
Cooking Time:15 Min + Freezing Time

Ingredients:

- 1 cup blueberries
- 1 cup pomegranate juice
- ¼ cup sugar
- ¼ tsp lemon zest

Directions:

1. Place the blueberries, lemon zest, and pomegranate juice in a saucepan over medium heat and bring to a boil. Simmer for 5 minutes or until the blueberries start to break down. Stir the sugar in ¼ cup of water until the sugar is dissolved. Place the blueberry mixture and the sugar water in your blender and blitz for 1 minute or until the fruit is puréed.
2. Pour the mixture into a baking pan. The liquid should come about ½ inch up the sides. Let the mixture cool for 30 minutes, and then put it into the freezer. Every 30 minutes for the next 2 hours, scrape the granita with a fork to keep it from freezing solid. Serve it after 2 hours, or store it in a covered container in the freezer.

Nutrition Info:

- Info Per Serving: Calories: 214;Fat: 0g;Protein: 1g;-Carbs: 54g.

Chive Ricotta Spread

Servings:4
Cooking Time:5 Minutes

Ingredients:

- 2 tbsp extra virgin olive oil
- 8 oz ricotta cheese, crumbled
- 2 tbsp fresh parsley, chopped
- ¼ cup chives, chopped
- Salt and black pepper to taste

Directions:

1. In a blender, pulse ricotta cheese, parsley, chives, salt, pepper, and olive oil until smooth. Serve.

Nutrition Info:

- Info Per Serving: Calories: 260;Fat: 12g;Protein: 12g;Carbs: 9g.

Pepperoni Fat Head Pizza

Servings:4
Cooking Time:35 Minutes

Ingredients:

- 2 tbsp olive oil
- 2 cups flour
- 1 cup lukewarm water
- 1 pinch of sugar
- 1 tsp active dry yeast
- ¾ tsp salt
- 1 tsp dried oregano
- 2 cups mozzarella cheese
- 1 cup sliced pepperoni

Directions:

1. Sift the flour and salt in a bowl and stir in yeast. Mix lukewarm water, olive oil, and sugar in another bowl. Add the wet mixture to the dry mixture and whisk until you obtain a soft dough. Place the dough on a lightly floured work surface and knead it thoroughly for 4-5 minutes until elastic. Transfer the dough to a greased bowl. Cover with cling film and leave to rise for 50-60 minutes in a warm place until doubled in size. Roll out the dough to a thickness of around 12 inches.
2. Preheat oven to 400 F. Line a round pizza pan with parchment paper. Spread the dough on the pizza pan and top with the mozzarella cheese, oregano, and pepperoni slices. Bake in the oven for 15 minutes or until the cheese melts. Remove the pizza from the oven and let cool slightly. Slice and serve.

Nutrition Info:

- Info Per Serving: Calories: 229;Fat: 7g;Protein: 36g;Carbs: 0.4g.

Sweet Spiced Pumpkin Pudding

Servings:6
Cooking Time: 0 Minutes

Ingredients:

- 1 cup pure pumpkin purée
- 2 cups unsweetened coconut milk
- 1 teaspoon ground cinnamon
- ¼ teaspoon ground nutmeg
- ½ teaspoon ground ginger
- Pinch cloves
- ¼ cup pure maple syrup
- 2 tablespoons chopped pecans, for garnish

Directions:

1. Combine all the ingredients, except for the chopped pecans, in a large bowl. Stir to mix well.
2. Wrap the bowl in plastic and refrigerate for at least 2 hours.
3. Remove the bowl from the refrigerator and discard the plastic. Spread the pudding with pecans and serve chilled.

Nutrition Info:

- Info Per Serving: Calories: 249;Fat: 21.1g;Protein: 2.8g;Carbs: 17.2g.

Two-cheese & Spinach Pizza Bagels

Servings:6
Cooking Time:20 Minutes

Ingredients:

- 2 tbsp olive oil
- 6 bagels, halved and toasted
- 2 green onions, chopped
- 1 cup pizza sauce
- ¼ tsp dried oregano
- 1 cup spinach, torn
- 1 ¼ cups mozzarella, grated
- ¼ cup Parmesan cheese, grated

Directions:

1. Preheat your broiler. Arrange the bagels on a baking sheet. Warm the olive oil in a saucepan over medium heat and sauté the green onions for 3-4 minutes until tender. Pour in the pizza sauce and oregano and bring to a simmer.
2. Spread the bagel halves with the sauce mixture and top with spinach. Sprinkle with mozzarella and Parmesan cheeses. Place under the preheated broiler for 5-6 minutes or until the cheeses melt.

Nutrition Info:

- Info Per Serving: Calories: 366;Fat: 8g;Protein: 20g;Carbs: 55g.

Citrus Cranberry And Quinoa Energy Bites

Servings:12
Cooking Time: 0 Minutes

Ingredients:

- 2 tablespoons almond butter
- 2 tablespoons maple syrup
- ¾ cup cooked quinoa
- 1 tablespoon dried cranberries
- 1 tablespoon chia seeds
- ¼ cup ground almonds
- ¼ cup sesame seeds, toasted
- Zest of 1 orange
- ½ teaspoon vanilla extract

Directions:

1. Line a baking sheet with parchment paper.
2. Combine the butter and maple syrup in a bowl. Stir to mix well.
3. Fold in the remaining ingredients and stir until the mixture holds together and smooth.
4. Divide the mixture into 12 equal parts, then shape each part into a ball.
5. Arrange the balls on the baking sheet, then refrigerate for at least 15 minutes.
6. Serve chilled.

Nutrition Info:

- Info Per Serving: Calories: 110;Fat: 10.8g;Protein: 3.1g;Carbs: 4.9g.

Chocolate-almond Cups

Servings:6
Cooking Time:10 Min + Freezing Time

Ingredients:

- ½ cup butter
- ½ cup olive oil
- ¼ cup ground flaxseed
- 2 tbsp cocoa powder
- 1 tsp vanilla extract
- 1 tsp ground cinnamon
- 2 tsp maple syrup

Directions:

1. In a bowl, mix the butter, olive oil, flaxseed, cocoa powder, vanilla, cinnamon, and maple syrup and stir well with a spatula. Pour into 6 mini muffin liners and freeze until solid, at least 2 hours. Serve and enjoy!

Nutrition Info:

- Info Per Serving: Calories: 240;Fat: 24g;Protein: 3g;Carbs: 5g.

Savory Cauliflower Steaks

Servings:4
Cooking Time:35 Minutes

Ingredients:

- 1 head cauliflower, cut into steaks
- 2 tbsp olive oil
- Salt and paprika to taste

Directions:

1. Preheat oven to 360 F.Line a baking sheet with aluminum foil. Rub each cauliflower steak with olive oil, salt, and paprika. Arrange on the baking sheet and bake for 10-15 minutes, flip, and bake for another 15 minutes until crispy.

Nutrition Info:

- Info Per Serving: Calories: 78;Fat: 7g;Protein: 1g;-Carbs: 4g.

Kid´s Marzipan Balls

Servings:6
Cooking Time:10 Minutes

Ingredients:

- ½ cup avocado oil
- 1 ½ cup almond flour
- ½ cup sugar
- 2 tsp almond extract

Directions:

1. Add the almond flour and sugar and pulse to your food processor until the mixture is ground. Add the almond extract and pulse until combined. With the processor running, stream in oil until the mixture starts to form a large ball. Turn off the food processor. With hands, form the marzipan into six 1-inch diameter balls. Press to hold the mixture together. Store in an airtight container in the refrigerator for up to 14 days.

Nutrition Info:

- Info Per Serving: Calories: 157;Fat: 17g;Protein: 2g;Carbs: 0g.

Amaretto Squares

Servings:6
Cooking Time:1 Hour 10 Minutes

Ingredients:

- 1 tsp olive oil
- Zest from 1 lemon
- 3/4 cup slivered almonds
- 2 cups flour
- 3/4 cup sugar
- 1 tsp baking powder
- ¼ tsp salt
- 3 eggs
- 2 tbsp Amaretto liqueur

Directions:

1. Preheat the oven to 280 F. Combine flour, baking powder, sugar, lemon zest, salt, and almonds in a bowl and mix well. In another bowl, beat the eggs and amaretto liqueur. Pour into the flour mixture and mix to combine.
2. Grease a baking sheet with olive oil and spread in the dough. Bake for 40-45 minutes. Remove from the oven, let cool for a few minutes, and cut diagonally into slices about ½-inch thick. Place the pieces back on the sheet, cut sides up, and bake for 20 more minutes. Let cool before serving.

Nutrition Info:

- Info Per Serving: Calories: 78;Fat: 1g;Protein: 2g;-Carbs: 14g.

Delicious Eggplant Balls

Servings:4
Cooking Time:55 Minutes

Ingredients:

- 3 tbsp olive oil
- 2 cups eggplants, chopped
- 3 garlic cloves, minced
- 2 eggs, whisked
- Salt and black pepper to taste
- 2 tbsp parsley, chopped
- ½ cup Pecorino cheese, grated
- ¾ cups panko breadcrumbs

Directions:

1. Preheat the oven to 360 F. Warm olive oil in a skillet over medium heat and sauté garlic and eggplants for 15 minutes. Mix cooked eggplants, eggs, salt, pepper, parsley, Pecorino cheese, and breadcrumbs in a bowl and form medium balls out of the mixture. Bake the balls for 30 minutes. Serve.

Nutrition Info:

- Info Per Serving: Calories: 230;Fat: 11g;Protein: 4g;Carbs: 6g.

Bruschetta With Tomato & Basil

Servings:4
Cooking Time:20 Minutes

Ingredients:

- 1 ciabatta loaf, halved lengthwise
- 2 tbsp olive oil
- 3 tbsp basil, chopped
- 4 tomatoes, cubed
- 1 shallot, sliced
- 2 garlic cloves, minced
- Salt and black pepper to taste
- 1 tbsp balsamic vinegar
- ½ tsp garlic powder

Directions:

1. Preheat the oven to 380 F. Line a baking sheet with parchment paper. Cut in half each half of the ciabatta loaf. Place them on the sheet and sprinkle with some olive oil. Bake for 10 minutes. Mix tomatoes, shallot, basil, garlic, salt, pepper, olive oil, vinegar, and garlic powder in a bowl and let sit for 10 minutes. Apportion the mixture among bread pieces.

Nutrition Info:

- Info Per Serving: Calories: 170;Fat: 5g;Protein: 5g;-Carbs: 30g.

Lebanese Spicy Baba Ganoush

Servings:4
Cooking Time:50 Minutes

Ingredients:

- 2 tbsp olive oil
- 2 eggplants, poked with a fork
- 2 tbsp tahini paste
- 1 tsp cayenne pepper
- 2 tbsp lemon juice
- 2 garlic cloves, minced
- Salt and black pepper to taste
- 1 tbsp parsley, chopped

Directions:

1. Preheat oven to 380 F. Arrange eggplants on a roasting pan and bake for 40 minutes. Set aside to cool. Peel the cooled eggplants and place them in a blender along with the tahini paste, lemon juice, garlic, cayenne pepper, salt, and pepper. Puree the ingredients while gradually adding olive oil until a smooth and homogeneous consistency. Top with parsley.

Nutrition Info:

- Info Per Serving: Calories: 130;Fat: 5g;Protein: 5g;-Carbs: 2g.

Grilled Pesto Halloumi Cheese

Servings:2
Cooking Time:9 Minutes

Ingredients:

- 1 tbsp olive oil
- 3 oz Halloumi cheese
- 2 tsp pesto sauce
- 1 tomato, sliced

Directions:

1. Cut the cheese into 2 rectangular pieces. Heat a griddle pan over medium heat. Drizzle the halloumi slices with and add to the pan. After about 2 minutes, check to see if the cheese is golden on the bottom. Flip the slices, top each with pesto, and cook for another 2 minutes, or until the second side is golden. Serve with tomato slices.

Nutrition Info:

- Info Per Serving: Calories: 177;Fat: 14g;Protein: 10g;Carbs: 4g.

Simple Artichoke Hearts With Aioli

Servings:4
Cooking Time:25 Minutes

Ingredients:

- 1 tbsp olive oil
- 1 red onion, chopped
- 2 garlic cloves, minced
- Salt and black pepper to taste
- 10 oz canned artichoke hearts
- 1 tsp lemon juice
- 1 cup light mayonnaise
- 2 tbsp thyme, chopped

Directions:

1. Warm the olive oil in a skillet over medium heat and cook the onion for 3 minutes. Stir in artichokes, salt, and pepper and stir-fry for 4-5 minutes; reserve. In a bowl, mix mayonnaise, lemon juice, and garlic. Sprinkle the artichokes with thyme and serve with aioli. Enjoy!

Nutrition Info:

- Info Per Serving: Calories: 120;Fat: 8g;Protein: 3g;-Carbs: 7g.

Salt & Pepper Toasted Walnuts

Servings:6
Cooking Time:20 Minutes

Ingredients:

- 2 tbsp olive oil
- 4 cups walnut halves
- Sea salt flakes to taste
- Black pepper to taste

Directions:

1. Preheat the oven to 250 F. In a bowl, toss the walnuts with olive oil, salt, and pepper to coat. Spread out the walnuts on a parchment-lined baking sheet. Toast for 10-15 minutes. Remove from the oven and allow to cool completely. Serve.

Nutrition Info:

- Info Per Serving: Calories: 193;Fat: 2g;Protein: 8g;-Carbs: 23g.

Apples Stuffed With Pecans

Servings:4
Cooking Time:55 Minutes

Ingredients:

- 2 tbsp brown sugar
- 4 apples, cored
- ¼ cup chopped pecans
- 1 tsp ground cinnamon
- ¼ tsp ground nutmeg
- ¼ tsp ground ginger

Directions:

1. Preheat oven to 375 F. Arrange the apples cut-side up on a baking dish. Combine pecans, ginger, cinnamon, brown sugar, and nutmeg in a bowl. Scoop the mixture into the apples and bake for 35-40 minutes until golden brown.

Nutrition Info:

- Info Per Serving: Calories: 142;Fat: 1.1g;Protein: 0.8g;Carbs: 36g.

Skillet Pesto Pizza

Servings:2
Cooking Time:10 Minutes

Ingredients:

- 1 tbsp butter
- 2 pieces of focaccia bread
- 2 tbsp pesto
- 1 medium tomato, sliced
- 2 large eggs

Directions:

1. Place a large skillet over medium heat. Place the focaccia in the skillet and let it warm for about 4 minutes on both sides until softened and just starting to turn golden. Remove to a platter. Spread 1 tablespoon of the pesto on one side of each slice. Cover with tomato slices. Melt the butter in the skillet over medium heat. Crack in the eggs, keeping them separated, and cook until the whites are no longer translucent and the yolk is cooked to desired doneness. Spoon one egg onto each pizza. Serve and enjoy!

Nutrition Info:

- Info Per Serving: Calories: 427;Fat: 17g;Protein: 17g;Carbs: 10g.

Easy No-bake Walnut & Date Oat Bars

Servings:6
Cooking Time:30 Minutes

Ingredients:

- ¼ cup butter, melted
- ¼ cup honey
- 12 dates, pitted and chopped
- 1 tsp vanilla extract
- ½ cup rolled oats
- ¾ cup sultanas, soaked
- 1 cup walnuts, chopped
- ¼ cup pumpkin seeds

Directions:

1. Place dates, vanilla, honey, oats, sultanas, butter, walnuts, and pumpkin seeds in a bowl and mix to combine. Transfer to a lined with parchment paper baking sheet and freeze for 30 minutes. Slice into bars and serve.

Nutrition Info:

- Info Per Serving: Calories: 280;Fat: 14g;Protein: 4g;Carbs: 15g.

APPENDIX A: Measurement Conversions

BASIC KITCHEN CONVERSIONS & EQUIVALENTS

DRY MEASUREMENTS CONVERSION CHART

3 TEASPOONS = 1 TABLESPOON = 1/16 CUP

6 TEASPOONS = 2 TABLESPOONS = 1/8 CUP

12 TEASPOONS = 4 TABLESPOONS = 1/4 CUP

24 TEASPOONS = 8 TABLESPOONS = 1/2 CUP

36 TEASPOONS = 12 TABLESPOONS = 3/4 CUP

48 TEASPOONS = 16 TABLESPOONS = 1 CUP

METRIC TO US COOKING CONVERSIONS

OVEN TEMPERATURES

120 °C = 250 °F

160 °C = 320 °F

180° C = 350 °F

205 °C = 400 °F

220 °C = 425 °F

LIQUID MEASUREMENTS CONVERSION CHART

8 FLUID OUNCES = 1 CUP = 1/2 PINT = 1/4 QUART

16 FLUID OUNCES = 2 CUPS = 1 PINT = 1/2 QUART

32 FLUID OUNCES = 4 CUPS = 2 PINTS = 1 QUART

= 1/4 GALLON

128 FLUID OUNCES = 16 CUPS = 8 PINTS = 4 QUARTS = 1 GALLON

BAKING IN GRAMS

1 CUP FLOUR = 140 GRAMS

1 CUP SUGAR = 150 GRAMS

1 CUP POWDERED SUGAR = 160 GRAMS

1 CUP HEAVY CREAM = 235 GRAMS

VOLUME

1 MILLILITER = 1/5 TEASPOON

5 ML = 1 TEASPOON

15 ML = 1 TABLESPOON

240 ML = 1 CUP OR 8 FLUID OUNCES

1 LITER = 34 FL. OUNCES

WEIGHT

1 GRAM = .035 OUNCES

100 GRAMS = 3.5 OUNCES

500 GRAMS = 1.1 POUNDS

1 KILOGRAM = 35 OUNCES

US TO METRIC COOKING CONVERSIONS

1/5 TSP = 1 ML

1 TSP = 5 ML

1 TBSP = 15 ML

1 FL OUNCE = 30 ML

1 CUP = 237 ML

1 PINT (2 CUPS) = 473 ML

1 QUART (4 CUPS) = .95 LITER

1 GALLON (16 CUPS) = 3.8 LITERS

1 OZ = 28 GRAMS

1 POUND = 454 GRAMS

BUTTER

1 CUP BUTTER = 2 STICKS = 8 OUNCES = 230 GRAMS = 8 TABLESPOONS

WHAT DOES 1 CUP EQUAL

1 CUP = 8 FLUID OUNCES

1 CUP = 16 TABLESPOONS

1 CUP = 48 TEASPOONS

1 CUP = 1/2 PINT

1 CUP = 1/4 QUART

1 CUP = 1/16 GALLON

1 CUP = 240 ML

BAKING PAN CONVERSIONS

1 CUP ALL-PURPOSE FLOUR = 4.5 OZ

1 CUP ROLLED OATS = 3 OZ 1 LARGE EGG = 1.7 OZ

1 CUP BUTTER = 8 OZ 1 CUP MILK = 8 OZ

1 CUP HEAVY CREAM = 8.4 OZ

1 CUP GRANULATED SUGAR = 7.1 OZ

1 CUP PACKED BROWN SUGAR = 7.75 OZ

1 CUP VEGETABLE OIL = 7.7 OZ

1 CUP UNSIFTED POWDERED SUGAR = 4.4 OZ

BAKING PAN CONVERSIONS

9-INCH ROUND CAKE PAN = 12 CUPS

10-INCH TUBE PAN =16 CUPS

11-INCH BUNDT PAN = 12 CUPS

9-INCH SPRINGFORM PAN = 10 CUPS

9 X 5 INCH LOAF PAN = 8 CUPS

9-INCH SQUARE PAN = 8 CUPS

Appendix B : Recipes Index

A

B

C

D

E

F

G

H

I

K

L

M

N

O

P

Q

R

S

T

V

W

Z

Made in United States
North Haven, CT
19 September 2023